# Mind-Boggling Facts from Ripley's

Once again, the hard-working crew from Ripley's has uncovered some of the most incredible wonders of the world! Here is another all-new collection of Ripley's phenomenal and remarkable oddities—all strange, all amazing, all true!

Did you know that—

- Robert Louis Stevenson (1850–1894) found the plot for *Dr. Jekyll and Mr. Hyde* in a nightmare!

- George Gershwin (1898–1937), one of America's greatest composers, was a professional pianist at 15!

- Dr. Adolph von Baeyer (1835–1917), a chemist in Berlin, Germany, who discovered barbituric acid—which gave us barbiturates—named his find not after an ingredient but in honor of a sweetheart named Barbara!

- Merry Christmas is a secretary in the fiscal control office at Mather Air Force Base in Sacramento, California—and always answers the telephone with, "Merry Christmas!"

**Ripley's Believe It or Not! titles**

Ripley's Believe It or Not! 28th Series
Ripley's Believe It or Not! 29th Series
Ripley's Believe It or Not! 30th Series
Ripley's Believe It or Not! Ghosts, Witches and ESP
Ripley's Believe It or Not! Great Disasters
Ripley's Believe It or Not! Stars, Space and UFOs

Published by POCKET BOOKS

Most Pocket Books are available at special quantity discounts for bulk purchases for sales promotions, premiums or fund raising. Special books or book excerpts can also be created to fit specific needs.

For details write or telephone the office of the Vice President of Special Markets, Pocket Books, 1230 Avenue of the Americas, New York, New York 10020. (212) 245-6400, ext. 1760.

# Ripley's Believe It or Not!

## 28TH SERIES

PUBLISHED BY POCKET BOOKS NEW YORK

Another *Original* publication of POCKET BOOKS

POCKET BOOKS, a Simon & Schuster division of
GULF & WESTERN CORPORATION
1230 Avenue of the Americas, New York, N.Y. 10020

ISBN: 0-671-46215-6

First Pocket Books printing May, 1978

10 9 8 7 6 5 4 3 2

# Preface

Looking for a way to introduce our readers to the 28th series of our *Believe It Or Not* Pocket Books, we checked through our research files to see if the number 28 had any significance. We found a wealth of information about events that took place on the 28th day of the month, and here are a few.

On August 28, 1565, St. Augustine, the nation's oldest city, was founded. On the same day in 1859, the first commercially productive oil well in the U.S. was discovered by Edwin L. Drake in Pennsylvania.

California was discovered on September 28, 1542, when Portuguese explorer Juan Rodriguez Cabrillo sailed from Mexico hoping to find prosperous cities and a water passage between the Atlantic and Pacific coasts. Cabrillo died shortly after exploring the San Diego Bay region, but his men continued up the coast exploring as far as present day Oregon.

The famous "Mutiny on the Bounty" took place on April 28, 1780, when Fletcher Christian took command of the *Bounty* and sailed it to Tahiti. He first set adrift the ship's Captain, William Bligh, together with eighteen sailors, in a small row boat. The *Bounty* reached Pitcairn Island and the row boat covered 3,618 miles before arriving at Timor, near Java.

On March 28, 1858, Eleazer A. Gardner of Philadelphia, patented the first Cable Car, and on the same day in 1895, construction began in Boston on America's first subway system.

The first commercial telephone switchboard in the world was installed at New Haven, Connecticut, with twenty-one subscribers, on January 28, 1878. It wasn't "Hello" that came over the wires of this new contraption, everyone called out "Ahoy".

An estimated one million people were present on October 28, 1886 when the Statue of Liberty was unveiled on Bedloe's Island, and the motion picture screen's most famous cartoon character, Mickey Mouse, made his film debut on September 28, 1928 in *Steamboat Willie*.

World War I began in Europe on June 28, 1914, when Archduke Franz Ferdinand of Austria was assassinated at Sarajevo. A little known fact about this event, is that he may not have died, if he had only had buttons on the tunic of his uniform. It appears that Franz Ferdinand was a very vain man, and he had been sewn into his uniform to assure him of a perfect fit. This made it very difficult to attend his wounds promptly, and he bled to death before his tunic could be cut off—Believe It Or Not!

—Research Department,
Ripley International Limited,
Toronto, Canada.

MALE WORSHIPERS OF THE GODDESS YELLAMA, in India, WEAR FEMALE CLOTHING --WHILE FEMALE WORSHIPERS WEAR MALE CLOTHING

THE **SLEEPING KNIGHT** Esch on the Sauer, Luxembourg, *NATURAL ROCK FORMATION*

ANNA MARIA PORTER (1781-1832) ENGLISH NOVELIST, PUBLISHED HER FIRST BOOK *AT THE AGE OF 11*

## A HOUSE DIVIDED

A HOME BUILT IN ZEYERN, IN NO. BAVARIA, BY BROTHERS KARL AND HANNES REBHUHN--*WHO COULDN'T AGREE ON ITS DESIGN*

Submitted by Emery F. Tobin, Vancouver, Wash.

A *SINGLE GRAVESTONE* IN AN UNUSED CEMETERY NEAR Joachimsthal, Germany, IS ALL THAT REMAINS OF THE VILLAGE OF MELLIN --*ALL INHABITANTS OF WHICH EMIGRATED* TO THE U.S. MORE THAN 100 YEARS AGO

A **RAM** ADDS AN ADDITIONAL SPIRAL SECTION TO ITS HORNS EACH YEAR

## TRINITY CHURCH

in St. Mary's City, Md., WAS BUILT WITH THE BRICKS OBTAINED IN THE DEMOLITION OF THE FIRST STATE HOUSE --*CONSTRUCTED WITH THOSE BRICKS IN 1676*

**CAVERN APARTMENT HOUSE**
A COLONY OF CAVE DWELLERS IN Tripoli, Libya, OCCUPIES A 4-STORY DWELLING IN A CAVE *50 FEET HIGH*

AN **IBO** TRIBESMAN IN NIGERIA, PAINTS HALF HIS BODY WHITE TO INDICATE *HE IS HALF BODY AND HALF SPIRIT*

**HENRY M. STANLEY**
(1841- 1904)
THE JOURNALIST WHO FOUND DAVID LIVINGSTONE IN AFRICA, DURING THE CIVIL WAR *SERVED WITH BOTH THE CONFEDERATE ARMY AND THE UNION NAVY*

**THE RULERS WHO ALWAYS DIED BY VIOLENCE !**
A CHIEF OF THE DINKA TRIBE OF THE SUDAN, AFRICA, WHEN IT BECAME OBVIOUS THAT HE WAS DYING OF OLD AGE OR ILLNESS, WAS *BURIED ALIVE*

**CHAMELEONS** WITH HORNS, ARE FOUND *ONLY IN THE BUGOYI REGION OF BURMA*

**THE SHOEMAKER WHO DID NOT STICK TO HIS LAST**
RUDOLF IPPISCH, of Austria, A SHOEMAKER BY TRADE, BECAME A WEALTHY SHIP-BUILDER, ORCHESTRA LEADER, OWNER OF MOVING-PICTURE THEATERS AND A BUILDER OF MOUNTAIN RAILWAYS AND HOTELS-- *YET CONTINUED OCCASIONALLY TO MAKE A PAIR OF SHOES BY HAND*

A **SAFETY PIN** INVENTED IN GREECE IN THE **8th** CENTURY B.C.

**FLOWERS** BLOOM IN PROFUSION ON THE COTENTIN PENINSULA OF FRANCE, ON THE THATCHED ROOFS OF FARM BUILDINGS

**FRANCIS B. SILBERG** A RABBI IN MILWAUKEE, WIS., AT THE AGE OF 32 SKIPPED ROPE CONTINUOUSLY FOR **4 HOURS, 10 MINUTES --** COMPLETING **35,000 JUMPS**

THE **LUCANUS CERVUS BEETLE** LIVES ONLY A FEW WEEKS-- *YET ITS LARVA LIVES 4 YEARS*

THE **GERMAN PRINCE ATLAS** INTO WHICH MAPS WERE BOUND IN 1666 -- *IS* **5 FEET, 10 INCHES HIGH** AND WEIGHS **275 POUNDS**

**CATHEDRAL ROCK**
ARDECHE CANYON, FRANCE,
*NATURAL FORMATION*

GENERAL
**ZACHARY
TAYLOR**
ALMOST LOST THE NOMINATION
FOR PRESIDENT OF THE U.S.
WHEN THE LETTER ASKING
HIM TO ACCEPT THE HONOR
WAS RETURNED UNOPENED
BY TAYLOR BECAUSE IT
CAME **"POSTAGE COLLECT"**

AN **UNFAITHFUL WIFE**
IN THE TUPURI
TRIBE OF AFRICA,
MUST WEAR
A BRASS RING
AROUND
HER NECK FOR
*THE REMAINDER
OF HER LIFE*

THE **CENTRAL SANCTUARY**
ATOP SACRED MT. TAI-SHAN. CHINA,
IS MERELY A WALL CONSTRUCTED
*AROUND SEVERAL BOULDERS
FOUND AT THE
MOUNTAIN'S PEAK*

THE **GATE
OF ARLES**
Nimes, France,
BUILT WITHOUT
MORTAR, HAS
ENDURED FOR
MORE THAN
2,100 YEARS

**THE GRAVES**
OF SKOLT LAPPS,
in Finland,
ARE ADORNED WITH
THE DEPARTED'S
*AXE AND BOAT
RUDDER*

GEORGE A.
**DILLMAN**
of Reading, Pa.,
SIMULTA-
NEOUSLY
BROKE 4
BLOCKS
OF ICE
WEIGHING
1,000 LBS.
*WITH HIS
ELBOW*

AUGUST 10
1974

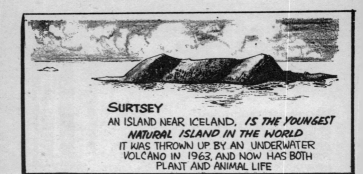

**SURTSEY**

AN ISLAND NEAR ICELAND, *IS THE YOUNGEST NATURAL ISLAND IN THE WORLD* IT WAS THROWN UP BY AN UNDERWATER VOLCANO IN 1963, AND NOW HAS BOTH PLANT AND ANIMAL LIFE

**CATHERINE de BOURBOULON** MARRIED THE SECRETARY OF THE FRENCH LEGATION IN THE U.S. AND WHEN HE WAS MADE FRENCH MINISTER TO CHINA *SHE BECAME THE FIRST EUROPEAN WOMAN TO ENTER AND LIVE IN PEKING*

**THE TALLEST NATURAL PYRAMID IN EUROPE** *A SPIRE OF EARTH* IN ITALY'S RENON MOUNTAINS IS 82 FEET TALL--PRESERVED FROM THE ICE AGE BY A STONE ON ITS PEAK--WHICH *PREVENTED THE EARTH'S EROSION BY RAINSTORMS*

**TRAIL RIDGE ROAD** LINKING ESTES PARK AND GRAND LAKE IN THE ROCKY MT. NATL. PARK, *MAINTAINS THE HIGHEST CONTINUOUS ALTITUDE OF ANY AUTOMOBILE HIGHWAY IN THE U.S.*

THE **GREBE** IS THE ONLY BIRD THAT DIVES INTO WATER FOR FISH -- *CARRYING ITS YOUNG ON ITS BACK*

THE **DINGO** THE AUSTRALIAN WILD DOG, IS THE ONLY ANIMAL NATIVE TO THAT COUNTRY *THAT EATS MEAT*

**THE PAVILION OF ART** in Zagreb, Yugoslavia, WAS MOVED 200 MILES TO ITS PRESENT SITE FROM BUDAPEST --*WHERE IT SERVED AS A PAVILION IN THE HUNGARIAN FAIR OF 1896*

THE REV. **FRANCIS XAVIER FAFARD** of St. Hyacinthe, Canada, WAS A PRIEST FOR **61** YEARS

15

## THE **WALKING TREASURE CHESTS**

WOMEN of Ladakh Province, Pakistan, WEAR A LEATHER BAND 2 FT. LONG AND 8 IN. WIDE STUDDED WITH TURQUOISES

*THAT REPRESENT ALL THEIR WORLDLY WEALTH*

**ORNATE TABLE** MADE BY THE GUÉRÉS OF AFRICA'S IVORY COAST FROM A SINGLE BLOCK OF MAHOGANY

**JOHN ADAMS** (1812-1860) A HERMIT OF CALIFORNIA'S SIERRA NEVADA MTS., CAPTURED GRIZZLY BEARS AND TAMED *THEM TO SERVE AS PACK ANIMALS*

THE **BODY** OF A HANGED MAN FOUND IN TOLLUND BOG DENMARK, IN 1950, WAS SO WELL PRESERVED THAT POLICE WERE CALLED --*YET THE MAN HAD BEEN EXECUTED 2,000 YEARS AGO*

A COTTON TREE IN BATHURST, GAMBIA, AFRICA, THAT HAS ENVELOPED A PIECE OF MACHINERY

**ONE PRONG** OF THE ANTLERS OF MALE REINDEER *PROTECTS AN EYE FROM DAMAGE IN THEIR FURIOUS BATTLES AT MATING TIME*

THE **STONE HAMMER** USED BY BLACK-SMITHS OF THE KYTCH TRIBE OF CENTRAL AFRICA *HAS NO HANDLE.* IT IS USED LIKE THE PESTLE OF A MORTAR

THE **COAT OF ARMS** OF MALANG, INDONESIA, HAS A 5-POINTED STAR AND A 5-SIDED COLUMN ON A 5-SIDED SHIELD-- *BECAUSE 5 IS CONSIDERED A SACRED NUMBER*

**LAFCADIO HEARN** (1850-1904) BECAME A PROFESSOR OF ENGLISH LITERATURE AT THE IMPERIAL UNIV. IN TOKYO, JAPAN, MARRIED A JAPANESE WOMAN AND ADOPTED A JAPANESE NAME --*YET NEVER LEARNED THE JAPANESE LANGUAGE*

AN **EMPEROR PENGUIN** SHIELDS ITS YOUNG FROM THE COLD BY HOBBLING ALONG WITH THE CHICK *BETWEEN ITS FEET*

A **CANDIDATE** IN RUANDA, AFRICA, SEEKING MEMBERSHIP IN A SECRET SOCIETY, MUST DEMONSTRATE *THAT HE CAN BREAK A SWORD WITH HIS TEETH*

**THE CHURCH OF KIRCHBÜHL** Switzerland, HOLDS SERVICES ONLY *3 TIMES EACH YEAR*

THE **OLD KILIAN FLOUR MILL** OF ALTLUNEN, AUSTRIA, WAS IN OPERATION FOR 92 YEARS, THEN WAS USED AS AN INN, AND *IS NOW A CHILDREN'S HOME*

**GAR MILLER** OF WENONAH, N.J. HAS A COLLECTION OF 150,000 BASEBALL CARDS-- *MANY, DATING BACK TO THE 1880's* Submitted by Jules H. Marr, Albuquerque, New Mexico

THE **NEW BRIDGE** OVER THE TAGUS RIVER, LISBON, PORTUGAL, RESTS UPON CAISSONS THAT DESCEND THROUGH **163 FT. OF MUD, SAND AND ROCK**

19

**THE FIRST MOVIE STAR!** FRED OTT, AN AIDE IN THOMAS ALVA EDISON'S LAB IN WEST ORANGE, N.J., GAVE THE FIRST MOVING PERFORMANCE IN FILM HISTORY--*A SNEEZE* -1893-

THE **COFFINS** IN WHICH CHIEFS OF THE **WANGATA** TRIBE OF THE **CONGO** ARE BURIED, *ARE CARVED IN THE SHAPES OF MEN AND WOMEN*

**TWIN VICTORY ARCHES** IN NAPLES, ITALY, CONSTRUCTED BY KING ALFONSO I OF NAPLES, *TO CELEBRATE 2 BATTLE VICTORIES IN 1423*

**CAPE PEMBROKE LIGHTHOUSE** IN THE FALKLAND ISLANDS, IS THE SOUTHERNMOST MANNED LIGHTHOUSE IN THE WORLD

THE MAN WHO BECAME A HERMIT FOR 50 YEARS BECAUSE HE WAS JILTED!

*JIMMY MASON* (1857-1942) of Great Canfield, England, WHEN HIS PROPOSAL WAS REJECTED BY THE GIRL HE LOVED, MOVED INTO A SHANTY SURROUNDED BY BARBED WIRE AND A FENCE --*AND NEVER LEFT IT UNTIL HIS DEATH*

A **MONUMENT** IN LE CAILAR, FRANCE, MARKS THE GRAVE OF SANGLIER --*A BULL FAMED FOR BRAVERY IN THE BULL-RING*

**2 HILLS** near Casteldelci, Italy, SHAPED BY EROSION TO RESEMBLE **EGYPT'S PYRAMIDS**

21

**THE FIRST POST OFFICE** IN NEW YORK CITY, WHICH UNTIL 1844 SERVED AS A CHURCH, HAD A SPECIAL MAIL WINDOW MARKED "LADIES"

**MAI SULE** SON OF THE RULER OF THE PABIRE TRIBE OF NIGERIA, CURED OF LEPROSY BY A CHRISTIAN MISSION, *RENOUNCED HIS SUCCESSION AND WEALTH, AND BECAME A CHRISTIAN PASTOR* (1951)

**TABLE LAMPS** IN AMERICA IN 1650, COMPRISED AN IRON CLAMP THAT HELD IN PLACE A *RUSH WICK*

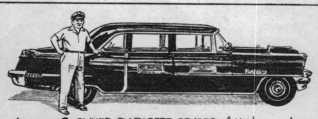

A **TAXICAB** OWNED BY ROBERT BENDER of Madison, Wis., *HAS BEEN DRIVEN 858,318 MILES.* HE BOUGHT IT SECONDHAND FOR $1500, 14 YEARS AGO. Submitted by Jules Marr, Albuquerque, N.M.

**"LIBERTAS"**
THE HOME OF ADAM TAS IN STELLENBOSCH, SO. AFRICA, WAS GIVEN THAT NAME—LATIN FOR "TAS" IS "FREE"—AS AN IRONIC GESTURE AFTER HE HAD *SPENT A YEAR IN PRISON FOR LIBELING A CORRUPT GOVERNOR*

THE **MAN** WHO WAS DEAD! FOR 3 DAYS!

**SAI BABA**
(1856-1918) of Shirdi, India, WAS PRONOUNCED DEAD IN 1886, WITH BOTH CIRCULATION AND BREATHING STOPPED COMPLETELY. AS PREPARATIONS FOR HIS FUNERAL WERE BEING MADE 3 DAYS LATER, IT WAS OBSERVED THAT HE WAS BREATHING— AND *HE LIVED ANOTHER 32 YEARS*

A **REPLICA** OF THE SPRING AND ALTAR OF LOURDES, FRANCE, *HAS BEEN ERECTED IN NYANZA, RUANDA, AFRICA*

**THE FLOATING ISLAND OF LAKE ALM** upper Austria, IT MOVES CONSTANTLY FROM SHORE TO SHORE

**JANE LEWSON** (1700-1816) of London, England, WAS SO FEARFUL OF CATCHING A COLD THAT **SHE NEVER WASHED** -- SHE LUBRICATED HER FACE AND HANDS WITH LARD -- AND LIVED TO THE AGE OF **116**

**MOBILE CLEANERS**
VACUUM WAGONS PARKED OUTSIDE OFFICE BUILDINGS, BY MEANS OF LONG HOSES, REMOVED DUST FROM CARPETS AND CURTAINS IN 1901

**"TO LOOK"** IN CHINESE, IS WRITTEN BY PLACING THE CHARACTER FOR "HAND" – 手 OVER THAT FOR "EYE" – 目

看

THE **OLD TOWER** OF GOSLAR, GERMANY, FORMERLY PART OF THE CITY WALL, WITH WALLS 21' 4" THICK, IS NOW A RESTAURANT

A **PRICELESS PAINTING** MADE OF HIS WIFE IN 1439, BY FLEMISH ARTIST JAN VAN EYCK, WAS DISCOVERED IN 1808, IN A FISH MARKET IN BRUGES, BELGIUM, BEING USED AS A TRAY ON WHICH *TO DISPLAY FISH*

A **FALLEN TREE** NEAR KARLHAFEN, GERMANY, THAT LOOKS LIKE A **PREHISTORIC MONSTER WITH GAPING JAWS**

**MANY CLIFFS** in N.W. China, ARE RIDDLED WITH CAVE HOMES *BUILT IN LAYERS, AND LINKED BY PATHS*

**JUVENILE DELINQUENCY**
BENITO MUSSOLINI, WHO BECAME ITALY'S DICTATOR, WAS TWICE EXPELLED FROM SCHOOL *FOR ASSAULTING FELLOW STUDENTS WITH A KNIFE*

A **LIMESTONE TABLET** FOUND AT KISH, IRAQ, AND DATED 3500 B.C., *IS THE OLDEST EXAMPLE OF PICTURE WRITING*

**JOHN LARNEY**
AN ESCAPEE FROM MASS. STATE PRISON TO COLLECT CIVIL WAR BOUNTIES *ENLISTED IN 93 REGIMENTS -- AND NEVER SERVED IN ANY OF THEM*

THE **WORLD'S BIGGEST HEARING AID** CREATED IN 1819 FOR KING JOHN VI of Portugal, *WAS AN ACOUSTIC-THRONE CHAIR...* COURTIERS KNELT AND SPOKE INTO THE LIONS' MOUTHS IN THE CHAIR'S HOLLOW ARMS

**HONORÉ de RACAN** (1589-1670) THE CELEBRATED FRENCH POET, COULD NOT PROPERLY PRONOUNCE *HIS OWN NAME.* HE HAD TROUBLE WITH THE LETTERS "R" AND "C"

A **DESK** CONSTRUCTED SHORTLY AFTER THE CIVIL WAR, ALSO SERVED *AS A BED AND A SINK*

THE **CHAPEL of ST.-ROCH** IN CHATELET, BELGIUM, WAS BUILT IN 1626, *AS AN ENTREATY FOR RELIEF FROM PESTILENCE*

**BENEDICT ARNOLD'S BOOT** IS DEPICTED ON AN UNMARKED MONUMENT AT SARATOGA, N.Y.— INDICATING THAT THE TRAITOR'S LEG, IN WHICH HE WAS TWICE WOUNDED IN BATTLE, *IS THE ONLY PART OF HIM WORTH HONORING*

**HENRY BURLING** (1801-1911) FIRST SETTLER OF FEATHERSTON, N.Z., LIVED TO THE AGE OF 110, AND AT HIS DEATH LEFT **600 DESCENDANTS**

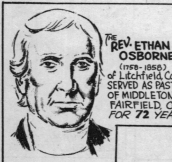

THE **REV. ETHAN OSBORNE** (1758-1858) of Litchfield, Conn., SERVED AS PASTOR OF MIDDLETON AND FAIRFIELD, CONN., FOR **72 YEARS**

**THE BELFRY** OF THE CHURCH OF OUR LADY, IN FRANKFORT ON THE MAIN, GERMANY, ORIGINALLY WAS A TOWER ON THE OLD CITY WALL

## WOMEN'S LIB--BULGARIAN STYLE

THE WEDDING RECEPTION IN BULGARIA, FEATURES A CONTEST IN WHICH THE BRIDE AND GROOM VIE TO SEE WHICH CAN BREAK OFF THE LARGEST SECTION OF A HUGE LOAF OF BREAD. *IF THE BRIDE WINS, SHE RULES THE HOUSEHOLD*

THE **FIRST TRAFFIC SIGNAL** INSTALLED OUTSIDE THE BRITISH PARLIAMENT IN 1868, WHICH LOOKED LIKE A RAILWAY SEMAPHORE AND HAD RED AND GREEN GAS LIGHTS-- *BLEW UP AND KILLED A POLICEMAN*

A **SELF-PORTRAIT** OF BEATRICE TURNER OF NEWPORT, R.I., A SOCIALITE ARTIST WHO PAINTED *1,000 PORTRAITS OF HERSELF*

THE **RED JACKET** - A CLIPPER-
SAILING FROM NEW YORK
TO LIVERPOOL, ENGLAND,
CROSSED THE ATLANTIC
IN 13 DAYS IN 1854,
*SETTING A SPEED RECORD
THAT WAS NEVER BROKEN*

A **STONE CROSS**
near Steinach,
Germany, MARKING
THE GRAVE OF A
GYPSY--**BURIED
ALIVE THERE
FOR LAWLESS
DEEDS**

**INDIAN WOMEN**
OF THE SAN BLAS TRIBE OF Panama,
PAINT BLACK LINES ON THEIR NOSES
*TO MAKE THEM APPEAR LONGER*

A **PAMPHLET**
PUBLISHED IN
PHILADELPHIA, PA.,
IN 1806, CARRYING
THE REPORT OF A
TRIAL OF BOOT
AND SHOEMAKERS
ON A CHARGE OF
**"CONSPIRACY TO
RAISE THEIR WAGES"**

THE **ROYAL BANNERS** OF DAHOMEY, AFRICA, WERE ALWAYS ORNAMENTED *WITH A HUMAN SKULL*

**ROBERT LOUIS STEVENSON** (1850-1894) FOUND THE PLOT FOR "DR. JEKYLL AND MR. HYDE" *IN A NIGHTMARE*

THE **PAGAN TEMPLE OF MITHRAS** LOCATED IN A CRYPT BENEATH THE CHURCH OF SAN CLEMENTE, IN ROME

**WOMEN** OF THE JOS PLATEAU, Togoland, Africa, ADVERTISE THEIR MARRIED STATE BY WEARING A *SMALL BUSTLE OF PLAITED STRAW*

**THE BRIDGE OF CHARENTON-LE-PONT** FRANCE, FIRST BUILT IN 52 B.C., HAS BEEN DESTROYED AND REBUILT **17 TIMES**

**STRINGS** OF **BEADS** ARE STILL USED BY THE KAYAN TRIBE OF BORNEO AS **MONEY**

**POLICEMEN** HAD TO COPE WITH SO MANY RIOTS IN 1857, THAT A PUBLICATION SUGGESTED THEY BE GIVEN SPECIAL UNIFORMS AND WEAPONS *BRISTLING WITH SHARP SPIKES*.

A **HOUSE** ON THE ISLAND OF TIMOR, INDONESIA, **IS BUILT FROM THE ROOF DOWN** *THE ROOF IS WOVEN FIRST AND THEN THE WALLS*

THE **FRUIT** OF THE AMBAGE TREE OF THE SUDAN, AFRICA, *LOOKS LIKE A FLYING BUTTERFLY*

THE **STATUE** of EMPEROR MARCUS AURELIUS IN ROME, ITALY, WAS USED IN THE MIDDLE AGES AS A GALLOWS-- *CRIMINALS WERE HANGED BY A ROPE LOOPED AROUND THE HORSE'S HEAD*

**GUGLIELMO CACCIA** (1568-1625) AN ITALIAN PAINTER, *WAS THE FATHER OF 5 NUNS*

THE **GREATER DWARF LEMUR** of Madagascar, *ALWAYS GIVES BIRTH TO TRIPLETS*

33

THE WORLD'S LARGEST ARCHIPELAGO LOCATED IN S.W. FINLAND, HAS 30,000 ISLANDS

THE ARCHED ENTRANCE TO THE PALACE OF THE RULER OF THERMESSOS, TURKEY, *IS THE ONLY STRUCTURE IN THAT ANCIENT PIRATES' HAVEN STILL STANDING*

EDWARD STEICHEN (1879-1973) THE FAMED PHOTOGRAPHER, SEEKING A PERFECT PRINT, *ONCE SPENT A FULL YEAR, AND TOOK 1,000 PHOTOS OF A WHITE CUP AND SAUCER*

A WHALING POT ACCEPTED BY THE MAORIS OF AUCKLAND, N.Z., IN EXCHANGE *FOR 1,000 ACRES OF LAND*

THE **GRAVESTONES** of the Ainu of Japan, ARE VERTICAL MARKERS-- WITH SPEAR-SHAPED TOPS FOR MEN, AND ROUNDED TOPS FOR WOMEN

THE **DEVIL PATROLMAN** WHO KEEPS ORDER IN KOLAHUN, LIBERIA, CONVINCES NATIVES HE HAS SUPERNATURAL POWERS BY PATROLLING THE JUNGLE PATHS ON STILTS-- *WEARING A MASK WITH NO EYE-SLITS*

**GEORGE WYTHE** (1726-1806) ONE OF THE SIGNERS OF THE DECLARATION OF INDEPENDENCE, WAS THE FIRST LAW PROFESSOR IN THE U.S. *--TEACHING AT THE COLLEGE OF WILLIAM AND MARY FROM 1779 TO 1790*

THE **CHURCH OF ST. MARY** IN LORENTZWEILER, LUXEMBOURG, IS LOCATED IN A *MOUNTAIN CAVE*

THE **LONG-TAILED SHEEP**
OF INDIA AND ASIA MINOR
PULL A SMALL
2-WHEELED CART WHICH
*SUPPORTS THEIR 10-LB. TAIL*

GEN· **CLAUDE-ANTOINE PREVAL** (1776-1853) WHO ENTERED THE FRENCH ARMY AT THE AGE OF **13** USING AN OLDER BROTHER'S BIRTH CERTIFICATE *ROSE TO THE RANK OF LIEUTENANT GENERAL*

**WOMEN** of Zeeland Province, Netherlands, WEAR BONNETS *THAT REVEAL THEIR RELIGION*

THE **LIGHTHOUSE** OF TRAVEMÜNDE, Germany, BUILT IN 1539, IS 114 FEET HIGH-- *YET IT WAS BUILT WITHOUT THE USE OF SCAFFOLDING*

**QUEEN MARY I** (1516-1558) of England, MARRIED KING PHILIP II of Spain, *32 YEARS AFTER BREAKING OFF HER ENGAGEMENT TO MARRY PHILIP'S FATHER, EMPEROR CHARLES V of GERMANY-- TO WHOM SHE HAD BEEN BETROTHED AT THE AGE OF 6*

**GEORGE GERSHWIN** (1898-1937) ONE OF AMERICA'S GREATEST COMPOSERS, WAS A PROFESSIONAL PIANIST *AT 15*

## THE GARDENER WHO WAS TOO GOOD FOR HIS EMPLOYER'S GOOD!

ANDRÉ LE NÔTRE (1613-1700) FAMED FRENCH GARDEN ARCHITECT, DESIGNED A GARDEN FOR NICOLAS FOUQUET, FRENCH SUPT. OF FINANCES, SO MAGNIFICENT THAT WHEN HE ENTERTAINED KING LOUIS XIV AT HIS ESTATE THE MONARCH BECAME SUSPICIOUS OF FOUQUET'S HONESTY, *AND 2 WEEKS LATER HAD HIM IMPRISONED FOR EMBEZZLEMENT*

A **PILLORY** PRESERVED AT THE CITY HALL OF SURSEE, IS THE *ONLY ONE REMAINING IN ALL SWITZERLAND*

**STATUETTES** FOUND IN TOMBS IN Changsha, China, REVEALED THAT THE CHINESE INVENTED STIRRUPS **1,675 YEARS AGO**

**RAFFLESIA HASSELTI** AN INSECT-EATING FLOWER OF MALAYA, IS 18 INCHES IN DIAMETER AND WEIGHS 14 POUNDS

**JIMMY CERTAIN**
of Fort Lauderdale, Fla.,
WHO WAS CRIPPLED BY
POLIO AS A CHILD,
"WALKED" 50 YARDS
BALANCED ON HIS HANDS
IN 27 SECONDS

Submitted by Jules Henry
Marr, Albuquerque, N.M.

**THE DYLE RIVER**
IN LOUVAIN, BELGIUM,
*FLOWS BENEATH THE CONVENT
OF THE AUGUSTINE SISTERS*

**KINNAREENAVA RESTAURANT**
IN Bangkok, Thailand,
LOCATED ON A PENINSULA
IN A LAKE, IS CONSTRUCTED IN THE SHAPE OF AN
*ANCIENT ROYAL BARGE*

## THE EXCLAMATION POINT

COMES FROM THE GREEK WORD "Io," MEANING: "I AM SURPRISED." THE "O" WAS FILLED IN AND PLACED UNDER THE "I" TO GIVE US: "!"

**THE WALLS** of Lucca, Italy, WERE PRESERVED IN 1866 WHEN THE CITY PURCHASED THEM *TO FORESTALL THEIR SALE BY THE ITALIAN GOVERNMENT AT AUCTION*

**CLAUDE de FORBIN** (1656-1733) A FRENCH MARINE OFFICER ATTACHED TO THE COURT OF THE KING OF SIAM, *BECAME ADMIRAL OF THE SIAMESE NAVY AND COMMANDER-IN-CHIEF OF THE SIAMESE ARMY*

**THE LONELY SENTRY** SOUTH-WEST AFRICA, *NATURAL STONE FORMATION*

**DR. ADOLPH von BAEYER** (1835-1917) A CHEMIST IN BERLIN, GERMANY, WHO DISCOVERED BARBITURIC ACID-- *WHICH GAVE US BARBITURATES*-- NAMED HIS FIND NOT AFTER AN INGREDIENT BUT IN HONOR OF A *SWEETHEART NAMED BARBARA*

THE **FRUIT** OF THE SNUFFBOX TREE OF AFRICA, IS SO HARD IT IS USED TO MAKE SNUFFBOXES-- *WHICH GIVES THE TREE ITS NAME*

**JOHN TYLER** (1790-1862) 10th PRESIDENT OF THE U.S., ENTERED THE COLLEGE OF WILLIAM AND MARY AT THE AGE OF 12

A **SPIRIT HOUSE** IS ERECTED AT HAZARDOUS CORNERS IN THAILAND *TO PLACATE THE EVIL SPIRITS THAT CAUSE TRAFFIC ACCIDENTS*

AN
**OVAHIMBA
WOMAN**
of S.W. Africa,
ANNOUNCES THAT
SHE IS MARRIED BY WEARING
*A LEATHER ROSETTE IN HER HAIR*

THE **FIRST MOTORCYCLE**
WAS INVENTED BY
GOTTLIEB DAIMLER IN
CANNSTADT, GERMANY,
IN 1885, ONLY 60 MILES
FROM WHERE KARL
BENZ CREATED HIS FIRST
PETROL-POWERED TRICYCLE
-*YET THEY NEVER MET*

THE **TREE HOUSES OF MALAYA**
SENOI TRIBESMEN BUILD THEIR
HOMES ON A PLATFORM RESTING
*ON THE BRANCHES OF A TREE*

**THE MEMORIAL
TO MARY
WASHINGTON**
THE MOTHER
OF GEORGE
WASHINGTON,
IN Fredericksburg,
Va., ERECTED
IN 1894,
*IS THE
FIRST
MONUMENT
FINANCED
BY WOMEN
TO HONOR
A WOMAN*

## THE OLD SOLDIER
CAPTAIN TCHGFIELONSKI
(1737-1847) of the Russian Army,
AFTER BEING DEPORTED TO
SIBERIA AND IMPRISONED
FOR **52 YEARS**, WAS
PARDONED BY CZAR NICHOLAS I
AND PROMOTED TO MAJOR
*AT THE AGE OF 106*

## AUSTRALIAN ABORIGINES
TO ANNOUNCE THAT THEY
ARE WIDOWERS SEEKING
ANOTHER WIFE, WEAR
**BLOBS OF MUD IN
THEIR BEARD**

A **RELIC**
EXHIBITED IN THE
ABBEY OF ST.
BARTHOLOMEW,
WUNSTORF,
GERMANY,
*IS THE
SHRUNKEN
HAND OF ST.
BARTHOLOMEW*

THE **ROCKING STONE**. Cornwall, England,
IT WEIGHS SEVERAL TONS-- *YET CAN BE
ROCKED WITH A SLIGHT PUSH*

**"Whiskey"** A FOX TERRIER LOST BY DRIVER GEOFF HANCOCK AT HAYS CREEK, AUSTRALIA, REJOINED HIS OWNER AT A TRUCK STOP AT MAMBREY CREEK 8 MONTHS LATER-- *HAVING TRAVELED 1,800 MILES OVER SOME OF AUSTRALIA'S ROUGHEST OUTBACK AREA*

Submitted by Emery F. Tobin, Vancouver, Wash.

THE REV. **STEPHEN T. BADIN** (1768-1853) A NATIVE OF FRANCE, WAS THE FIRST CATHOLIC PRIEST ORDAINED IN THE U.S. *--TAKING HIS VOWS IN BALTIMORE, MD., IN 1793, AND SERVING IN THE WILDERNESS FOR 60 YEARS*

# HAJIKAMI

A JAPANESE GRAND-CHAMPION WRESTLER WAS SO STRONG AND SKILLFUL, THAT HE TIED A WHITE HAWSER AROUND HIS WAIST AND CHALLENGED *ANYONE TO PUT A FINGER ON IT.* NO ONE EVER DID AND JAPANESE GRAND CHAMPIONS STILL WEAR A WHITE ROPE IN HIS MEMORY 1,100 YEARS LATER

**ELEPHANT ROCK**
Fire State Park, Nev.
NATURAL STONE FORMATION

AN **ANTHILL**
NEAR LAGOS,
NIGERIA,
*SHAPED LIKE
A CHURCH*

**JAMES GORDON BENNETT, Jr.**
THE NEWSPAPER EDITOR WHO SENT
STANLEY TO AFRICA TO FIND LIVINGSTONE,
*WAS CONVINCED HE WOULD NOT
LIVE BEYOND HIS 77th BIRTHDAY.*
HE SANK INTO A COMA IN
PARIS, FRANCE, ON MAY 10, 1918--
*HIS 77th BIRTHDAY--
AND DIED 4 DAYS LATER*

A **FOUNTAIN**
IN THE MOSQUE OF
IBN TULUN, IN
CAIRO, EGYPT,
WAS ORIGINALLY
DESIGNED BY
SULTAN
IBN TULUN
*AS HIS
TOMB*

## JOSEPH PRIESTLEY

(1733-1804)
THE ENGLISH CHEMIST,
CREATED SODA
WATER AFTER
HE BECAME INTERESTED
IN THE FORMATION
OF GASES
DURING FERMENTATION
WHEN HE
*MOVED*
*NEXT DOOR*
*TO A BREWERY*

THE
**TOWER**
A
STANDARD
CONFECTION
IN CREMONA,
ITALY, IS A
MINIATURE
OF THE
WEDDING-
CAKE BAKED
AT THE
WEDDING
OF THE
DAUGHTER
OF THE
DUKE OF
CREMONA
**534**
**YEARS**
**AGO**

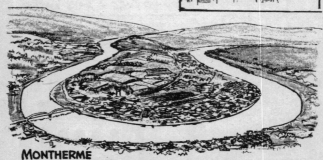

**MONTHERMÉ**
A TOWN IN FRANCE, IS LOOPED BY THE RIVER MEUSE

THE **TEMPLE OF THE GOD OF FOOD** in Chobar Nepal, IS DECORATED WITH COUNTLESS OFFERINGS OF *POTS AND PANS*

## HANNAH SIMPSON GRANT

WAS IN WASHINGTON, D.C. MANY TIMES WHILE HER SON, ULYSSES S. GRANT, WAS PRESIDENT OF THE U.S. (1869-1877) *BUT NEVER VISITED THE WHITE HOUSE*

**NATIVES** of New Guinea, OFTEN SMOKE THEIR HOME-MADE CIGARETS *FROM THE SIDE*

**27764**

**MR. AND MRS. ROBERT C. LEWIS** OF ESTILL SPRINGS, TENN., HAVE IDENTICALLY NUMBERED BIRTH CERTIFICATES, *YET HE WAS BORN IN TENNESSEE AND SHE WAS BORN IN VIRGINIA*

**ST. CATHERINE'S CHURCH** in Zagreb Yugoslavia, WAS CONSTRUCTED IN 1632 *AS A REPLICA OF THE CHURCH OF JESUS IN ROME, ITALY*

A **GRANITE COFFIN** IN A QUARRY AT ASWAN, EGYPT, BECAUSE THE PHARAOH FOR WHOM IT WAS BEING PREPARED WAS SUDDENLY DEPOSED, HAS REMAINED UNFINISHED FOR **3,800 YEARS**

## STENDHAL
### (1783 - 1842)
THE FRENCH AUTHOR, WHO WROTE "THE RED AND THE BLACK" AND "THE CHARTERHOUSE OF PARMA," ACHIEVED WORLD RECOGNITION AS A MAJOR LITERARY FIGURE *AFTER HE HAD BEEN DEAD FOR 100 YEARS*

**FLECHTINGEN CASTLE**
NEAR MAGDEBURG, GERMANY, WAS UNDER CONSTRUCTION FOR 400 YEARS

**THE BEE'S APARTMENT HOUSE** THE CARPENTER BEE OF AUSTRALIA, DEPOSITS ITS EGGS IN TUNNELS IT DIGS IN A TREE BRANCH --DIGGING TUNNELS *15 INCHES LONG TO PROVIDE INDIVIDUAL QUARTERS FOR EACH EGG*

**A ZEBRA'S STRIPES** *ARE AS INDIVIDUAL AS HUMAN FINGERPRINTS* NO TWO ZEBRAS ARE STRIPED EXACTLY ALIKE

**A CALF** BORN WITH 5 LEGS, 2 TAILS AND 2 UDDERS
Submitted by J. O'SULLIVAN Bayswater, W. Australia

**DR. SALO FINKELSTEIN** THE POLISH MATHEMATICAL WIZARD, WAS EMPLOYED BY HIS GOVERNMENT'S TREASURY DEPARTMENT TO *REPLACE 40 TRAINED MEN AND 40 CALCULATING MACHINES*

**THE FINGERS OF FATE** A STONE HAND-- NATURAL ROCK FORMATION IN MALI, AFRICA, WITH FINGERS POINTING TO HEAVEN

**THE "LIFE LINE"** --A 40-FOOT CABIN CRUISER-- THAT SAILED THE COOS RIVER, IN OREGON, FOR YEARS, WAS A FLOATING CHAPEL

## A WINDMILL
THE TALLEST STRUCTURE IN NEW AMSTERDAM, IN 1660 WAS INSTRUMENTAL IN MAKING NEW YORK "THE GREATEST CITY IN THE WORLD," BECAUSE IT WAS USED TO PRODUCE FLOUR AND BREAD--AND NEW AMSTERDAM, BY LAW, WAS THE ONLY PORT ALLOWED TO EXPORT THOSE PRODUCTS

### CHARLES V. BOULTON
A U.S. ARMY STAFF SERG. IN WORLD WAR II, PICKED UP A WORLD-WAR I DRAFT FILE FROM A PILE BEING BURNED IN 1942, AND FOUND IT WAS THAT OF A FRIEND: EDWARD MELICK, OF NELIGH, NEBRASKA-- ONE OF 24,234,021 SUCH CARDS BEING DESTROYED!

### GONGS
MADE BY THE MAORIS OF NEW ZEALAND, WERE FASHIONED INSIDE A TREE SO THE REMAINDER OF THE TRUNK SERVED AS A SOUNDING BOARD

### THE PILLAR OF DEATH
near Rosenburg Castle, Upper Austria, MARKS THE SPOT WHERE 300 MEN, WOMEN AND CHILDREN STRICKEN IN THE PLAGUE OF 1620, GATHERED TO AWAIT DEATH

51

**MERRY CHRISTMAS** IS A SECRETARY IN THE FISCAL CONTROL OFFICE AT MATHER AIR FORCE BASE IN SACRAMENTO, CALIF.-- AND ALWAYS ANSWERS THE TELEPHONE WITH, "MERRY CHRISTMAS"

THE **DOMINICAN CHAPEL OF ST. NICHOLAS** in Stellenbosch, So. Africa, ORIGINALLY WAS *A WINE CELLAR*

**EDWARD LIVINGSTON** (1764-1836) FROM 1800 TO 1803, SERVED AS MAYOR OF NEW YORK CITY AND AS DISTRICT ATTORNEY *SIMULTANEOUSLY*

A **ROCKING STONE** AT INDIAN CAVE, PULASKI COUNTY, MO., WEIGHING MANY TONS, HAS BALANCED PRECARIOUSLY OVER THE CAVE'S ENTRANCE *FOR CENTURIES*

## $500.00
### Life Insurance
### In Case of Death if You Use This Medicine

**ADVERTISEMENT** IN THE EARLY 1900'S OF A PATENT MEDICINE COMPANY IN AKRON, OHIO, THAT OFFERED PURCHASERS A $500 LIFE INSURANCE POLICY AGAINST FATAL RESULTS FROM ITS USE

**LOUIS JACQUES MANDE DAGUERRE** INVENTOR OF THE DAGUERREOTYPE, THE FIRST GLASS PLATE PHOTOGRAPHS, HAD AN *AVERSION TO HAVING HIS OWN PICTURE TAKEN*

### GRYLLOBLATTA CAMPODEIFORMIS
A WINGLESS ORTHOPTERAN INSECT, CAN SURVIVE IN A FROZEN STATE IN ARCTIC REGIONS FOR MONTHS--YET *DIES IF EXPOSED TO THE WARMTH OF A HUMAN HAND*

THE **STONE IGUANA** WHICH GAVE GUANA, ONE OF THE VIRGIN ISLANDS, ITS NAME

THE **LARGE PAPER NAUTILUS** OF AUSTRALIA, HAS A SHELL 9½ INCHES LONG

THE **COWBOY OF THE SEA** COLIN OSTLE WHILE CATCHING BAIT FISH IN KING GEORGE SOUND, W. Australia, *LASSOED A 3,234-POUND SHARK*

**WILLIAM COX** WHO WAS UNJUSTLY CASHIERED OUT OF THE U.S. NAVY IN THE WAR OF 1812 BECAUSE HE LOST THE FRIGATE "CHESAPEAKE," WAS COMMISSIONED A 3d LIEUTENANT *78 YEARS AFTER HIS DEATH*

A **RAFT** ON THE KABUL RIVER, AFGHANISTAN, WHICH IS SUPPORTED BY INFLATED ANIMAL SKINS *AND CARRIES A LOAD OF 12 PASSENGERS*

**KING EDWARD VIII** of England, IS THE ONLY BRITISH MONARCH WHO WROTE *AN AUTOBIOGRAPHY*

**ROBERT S. SVOB** A HALFBACK ON THE FOOTBALL TEAM OF JEROME H.S. IN ARIZONA, *PLACEKICKED A FOOTBALL 300 YARDS*

Oct. 1936

*THE* **CATERPILLAR** OF THE THORN MOTH MAINTAINS AN UPRIGHT POSITION BESIDE A PLANT BRANCH BY *SPINNING A SILK THREAD FROM THE BRANCH TO ITS HEAD*

A **GATE** AT LLOYD LAKE IN SAN FRANCISCO'S GOLDEN GATE PARK, ORIGINALLY STOOD IN FRONT OF THE HOME OF A.N.TOWNE -- *WHICH WAS WRECKED IN THE EARTHQUAKE OF 1906*

**THE OLD CUSTOM HOUSE**
BUILT IN NEW YORK CITY IN 1790,
WAS ORIGINALLY INTENDED TO
BE QUARTERS FOR THE
*PRESIDENT OF THE UNITED
STATES, THE U.S. SENATE, THE
HOUSE OF REPRESENTATIVES
AND VISITING STATESMEN*

**HENRY KNOX**
WHO SERVED AS GEORGE
WASHINGTON'S COMMANDER OF
ARTILLERY, WAS AN AMATEUR
SOLDIER WHO LEARNED
ARTILLERY USAGE READING
*MILITARY BOOKS IN
HIS BOSTON BOOKSTORE*

**WILLIAM FRED COOK**
(1840-1890)
of Leicester, England,
WAS BORN ON A
THURSDAY-- WAS MARRIED
ON A THURSDAY--
NEVER BECAME
ILL ON ANY
DAY BUT
THURSDAY--
*AND DIED
ON A
THURSDAY*

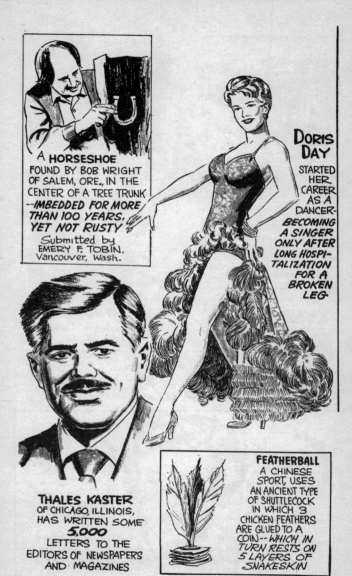

A **HORSESHOE** FOUND BY BOB WRIGHT OF SALEM, ORE., IN THE CENTER OF A TREE TRUNK --*IMBEDDED FOR MORE THAN 100 YEARS, YET NOT RUSTY*

Submitted by EMERY F. TOBIN, Vancouver, Wash.

**DORIS DAY** STARTED HER CAREER AS A DANCER- *BECOMING A SINGER ONLY AFTER LONG HOSPITALIZATION FOR A BROKEN LEG-*

**THALES KASTER** OF CHICAGO, ILLINOIS, HAS WRITTEN SOME **5,000** LETTERS TO THE EDITORS OF NEWSPAPERS AND MAGAZINES

**FEATHERBALL** A CHINESE SPORT, USES AN ANCIENT TYPE OF SHUTTLECOCK IN WHICH 3 CHICKEN FEATHERS ARE GLUED TO A COIN-- *WHICH IN TURN RESTS ON 5 LAYERS OF SNAKESKIN*

THE RUINS ON THE ISLAND OF COS, GREECE, HOME OF HIPPOCRATES, THE FATHER OF MEDICINE, ARE VISITED EACH YEAR BY A GROUP OF FRENCH PHYSICIANS WHO *RENEW THEIR HIPPOCRATIC OATH AS GIRLS DRESSED IN ANCIENT GRECIAN GARB DANCE TO THE TUNE OF A FLUTE*

**ZACHARY ZZZZRA**
IS THE LAST NAME IN THE SAN FRANCISCO TELEPHONE DIRECTORY 1975

HERE 'TIZ

**THE ARMY OF GRAYBEARDS**
COL· CALLIÈRES de l'ESTANG AT THE AGE OF 66 RECRUITED, DRILLED AND COMMANDED FOR THE REGULAR FRENCH ARMY A BATTALION OF 1,000 INFANTRYMEN-- *THE YOUNGEST, 60 YEARS OF AGE AND THE OLDEST, 90*

**MRS. A. GOODWIN** OF NEWTON, SYDNEY, AUSTRALIA, BECAME THE MOTHER OF TWIN BOYS *-BORN 56 DAYS APART AND IN DIFFERENT YEARS --* DENIS WAS BORN DEC.16,1952 AND DAVID ON FEB.10,1953

**JUANITO APINANI** A 19th-CENTURY MATADOR FROM SPAIN, THRILLED CROWDS BY USING A LANCE TO LEAP OVER A CHARGING BULL

A **FIR TREE** IN Vyzne Ruzbachy, Slovakia, GROWING FROM A POOL FED BY **HOT SPRINGS**

**5 BLUE MINARETS** IN HERAT, AFGHANISTAN, ARE ALL THAT REMAIN OF 2 MOSQUES *THAT STOOD ON THE SITE 500 YEARS AGO*

THE **WASHINGTON SQUARE ARCH**
IN NEW YORK CITY,
WAS ORIGINALLY CONSTRUCTED,
IN 1889, **OF WOOD.**
IT WAS TOPPED BY A WOODEN
FIGURE OF WASHINGTON--
*11 FEET TALL*

**HIJMAR**
HOLY MAN, IN BENARES, INDIA,
HAS HELD HIS LEFT ARM IN
THE SAME POSITION FOR
*12 YEARS*

THE CHURCH OF EL CRISTO de la LUZ
Toledo, Spain,
WAS BUILT AS A CHRISTIAN CHURCH--
CONVERTED INTO A MOSQUE IN 980, AND
*FINALLY BECAME A CHURCH AGAIN
WHEN SPAIN CONQUERED THE MOORS IN 1085*

MODERN
ARM-
CHAIRS
ARE CARVED
BY THE
NGONIS OF
CENT. AFRICA,
FROM A
SOLID
BLOCK OF
WOOD

## THE CORONATION STONE
KINGSTON, ENGLAND,
UPON IT WERE CROWNED
SEVERAL OF THE EARLIEST
SAXON KINGS OF ENGLAND

## FASHIONABLE WOMEN
IN ENGLAND IN THE
LATE 19th CENTURY,
ACHIEVED PINK CHEEKS,
RED LIPS AND PERFECT
EYEBROWS BY
*TATTOOING*

## JAMES KNOX POLK
THE 11th PRESIDENT
OF THE UNITED STATES,
HAD A UNIQUE
RECORD OF
FULFILLING
EVERY PLEDGE
MADE IN HIS
CAMPAIGN--
*YET HE WAS
THE FIRST
PRESIDENT
TO REFUSE
TO RUN FOR
REELECTION*

## A GEODE
STONE MARKED
WITH A NATURAL
*OUTLINE OF THE
UNITED STATES*
Submitted by
Clyde G. Beasley,
Yuma, Arizona.

**ROMAN SOLDIERS**
CARRIED THEIR POSSESSIONS
--INCLUDING COOKING UTENSILS--
TIED TO THEIR SPEARS

*The* **CHURCH OF TSCHERNIHEIM**
Carinthia, Austria, IS THE ONLY
STRUCTURE STANDING IN THE
VILLAGE DESERTED BY ALL ITS
INHABITANTS 96 YEARS AGO

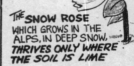

*The* **SNOW ROSE**
WHICH GROWS IN THE
ALPS, IN DEEP SNOW,
*THRIVES ONLY WHERE
THE SOIL IS LIME*

**PANAMA HATS**
*ARENT MADE IN PANAMA.*
THEY ARE MADE IN
ECUADOR, COLOMBIA AND
PERU, BUT GOT THEIR
NAME BECAUSE THE
FORTY-NINERS, ON THEIR
WAY TO CALIFORNIA,
FOUND THEM FOR SALE
IN PANAMA CITY

**ARCHWAY**
IN STORNOWAY, SCOTLAND, MADE
BY LINKING 2 WHALEBONES

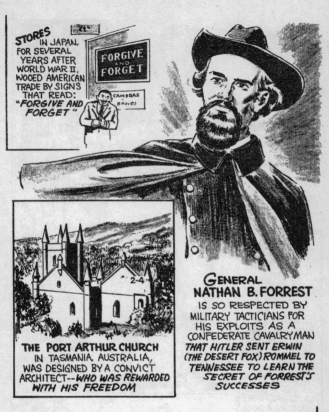

**STORES** IN JAPAN, FOR SEVERAL YEARS AFTER WORLD WAR II, WOOED AMERICAN TRADE BY SIGNS THAT READ: *"FORGIVE AND FORGET"*

FORGIVE AND FORGET

CAMERAS RADIOS

**THE PORT ARTHUR CHURCH** IN TASMANIA, AUSTRALIA, WAS DESIGNED BY A CONVICT ARCHITECT--*WHO WAS REWARDED WITH HIS FREEDOM*

**GENERAL NATHAN B. FORREST** IS SO RESPECTED BY MILITARY TACTICIANS FOR HIS EXPLOITS AS A CONFEDERATE CAVALRYMAN *THAT HITLER SENT ERWIN (THE DESERT FOX) ROMMEL TO TENNESSEE TO LEARN THE SECRET OF FORREST'S SUCCESSES*

**MANTLE COMBS** PROPEL THEMSELVES IN ZIGZAG FASHION BY OPENING AND CLOSING THEIR DOUBLE VALVES--LIKE HANDS CLAPPING

AN *ICE MONUMENT* APPEARS ON THE KAMZIK RIVER, IN SLOVAKIA, *EVERY WINTER*

**JOHN BRALLIER** THE NATION'S FIRST PROFESSIONAL FOOTBALL PLAYER, WHO WAS A QUARTERBACK FOR THE LATROBE, PA., TEAM, IN 1895, *WAS 5 FEET, 6 INCHES TALL AND WEIGHED 125 POUNDS*

A **TOTEM POLE** CARVED BY THE ASMAT TRIBESMEN OF ERMASONA, NEW GUINEA, *DEPICTS THE ENEMIES THEY HAVE SLAIN IN BATTLE*

A **STATUE** OVER A WELL IN COLMAR, FRANCE HONORS A DOG THAT SAVED ITS OWNER BY AWAKENING HIM IN HIS *BURNING HOME*

**SIGN** IN Carmel, Calif., ON A ROAD THAT LEADS TO THE RANCHO CANADA GOLF CLUB AND THE COMMUNITY CHURCH OF MONTEREY

Submitted by Jules H. Marr, Albuquerque, N.M.

## THE CHURCH OF ST. CECILIA

in Rome, Italy, WAS BUILT OVER THE HOUSE *IN WHICH ST. CECILIA LIVED*

"I CANNOT TELL A LIE"
the "Boss" Lunch Milk Biscuit
is the best in America

### ADVERTISEMENTS

IN THE LATE 19TH CENTURY, OFTEN USED UNWITTING *ENDORSEMENTS OF THEIR PRODUCTS BY U.S. PRESIDENTS*

### RULES OF THIS TAVERN

Four pence a night for Bed
Six pence with Supper
No more than five to sleep in one bed
No Boots to be worn in bed
Organ Grinders to sleep in the Wash house
No dogs allowed upstairs
No Beer allowed in the Kitchen
No Razor Grinders or Tinkers taken in

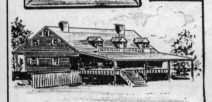

**BEHAVIOR RULES** POSTED IN 1850, IN MADISON COTTAGE, A ROADHOUSE LOCATED AT BROADWAY AND 23d STREET IN NEW YORK CITY

THE **BRONZE "PURSE"**
A RING FROM WHICH DANGLES THE RING MONEY OF THE PERIOD, WAS FOUND IN A GRAVE AT WOLLISHOFEN, SWITZERLAND, WHERE IT HAD LAIN FOR *MORE THAN 2,800 YEARS*

Paolo
DAGOMARI

(1281-1372) AN ITALIAN MATHEMATICIAN, CONCEIVED THE USE OF THE COMMA
*TO SEPARATE LARGE FIGURES INTO UNITS OF THREE*

J.P.
MORGAN
.. THE NEW YORK CITY
FINANCIER,
CLAIMED DESCENT
FROM SIR
HENRY MORGAN
THE PIRATE ... PAINTED
EACH OF HIS YACHTS
BLACK ... AND
*ALWAYS
NAMED THEM
"CORSAIR"*

**THE SHIP THAT BECAME A SHRIMP COCKTAIL**
"THE IMPERIAL" A STEAMSHIP DOCKED IN NEW ORLEANS, LA, SUDDENLY SANK BECAUSE THE OAKUM IN HER SEAMS HAD BEEN *EATEN OUT BY SHRIMP*

**THE FIRST PRINTING PRESS IN AMERICA** SET UP BY STEPHEN DAY IN CAMBRIDGE, MASS., *IN 1640*

**FLAG WASPS** Icaria Variegata, BUILD A SERIES OF PAPER-LIKE NESTS *WHICH STAND OUT LIKE FLAGS FROM A TREE BRANCH*

**CHILDREN** of the Nanay Tribe, Siberia, TRAVEL TO AND FROM THEIR DISTANT SCHOOL ON SKIS --- **PULLED BY DOGS**

**THE TOWN HALL**
OF BRAUNSBERG, POLAND, HAS AN INSCRIPTION IN LATIN THAT READS: "This house hates and loves, punishes, defends and honors laziness, industry, evil deeds, right, and rectitude"

John
**RUTLEDGE**
(1739-1800),
APPOINTED CHIEF JUSTICE OF THE U.S. SUPREME COURT BY GEORGE WASHINGTON, WAS REJECTED BY THE U.S. SENATE--*AFTER HE HAD ALREADY PRESIDED OVER THE COURT FOR 4 MONTHS*

**WILLIAM BANTING** --
A 203-LB. UNDERTAKER, IN LONDON, ENGLAND, *WAS THE FIRST PERSON PUT ON A SCIENTIFIC DIET TO LOSE WEIGHT*
HE DROPPED TO 153 LBS. ON A REDUCED CARBOHYDRATE INTAKE PRESCRIBED BY AN EAR SPECIALIST
- 1862 -

THE MOST DARING MATADOR IN ALL HISTORY *CARLOS ARRUZA,* DURING A BULLFIGHT IN MALAGA, SPAIN, RESTED AN ARM ON THE FOREHEAD OF A 1,600-LB. BULL, *AND HELD THE BEAST'S HORN IN HIS MOUTH!* A TOSS OF THE BULL'S HEAD WOULD HAVE GORED THE MATADOR'S THROAT (AUG. 27, 1945)

A **MOCK CASTLE** 70 FEET HIGH, BUILT IN EDGEHILL, ENGLAND, TO COMMEMORATE THE FIRST BATTLE OF THE ENGLISH CIVIL WAR -- *FOUGHT IN 1642*

**GIOACCHINO ROSSINI** THE ITALIAN COMPOSER, WROTE 38 OPERAS DURING THE FIRST 37 YEARS OF HIS LIFE, *BUT NEVER WROTE ANOTHER OPERA, ALTHOUGH HE LIVED ANOTHER 39 YEARS*

## PRESIDENT CHESTER ALAN ARTHUR
### (1830-1886)

WHO, IN 1883, SIGNED THE BILL CREATING CIVIL SERVICE, HAD BEEN REMOVED FROM HIS POST AS COLLECTOR OF THE PORT OF NEW YORK *FOR GIVING JOBS TO PARTY WORKERS*

## WORM'S HEAD PENINSULA

IN So. Wales, England, WAS GIVEN THAT NAME BECAUSE ITS OUTLINE *MAKES IT LOOK LIKE A SEA SERPENT*

## THE BATHTUB

USED IN THE WHITE HOUSE BY PRESIDENT WILLIAM HOWARD TAFT, WAS SO HUGE, TO HOLD HIS HEFTY BULK, THAT *4 WORKMEN ONCE SAT IN IT COMFORTABLY*

**FINGERPRINTS** AS A MEANS OF IDENTIFICATION, WERE FIRST USED BY WILLIAM HERSCHEL, AT JUNGIPUR, INDIA, ON A CONTRACT 117 YEARS AGO

**JOHN D. BANKS** OF SPANISH FORK, UTAH, HAS LIVED IN THE HOUSE IN WHICH HE WAS BORN *FOR 90 YEARS* Submitted by Ray Banks Fontana, Calif.

THE **TREE TOAD** of Martinique, CLIMBS TREES WITH ITS YOUNG CLINGING TO ITS BACK

**STONE** SHAPED LIKE A *BOOT* Submitted by Shane Fazzio, Loveland, Colo.

AN **AZTEC STONE CALENDAR** AT THE PYRAMID OF THE SUN IN MEXICO CITY, MEXICO, WEIGHS 20 TONS AND COVERS THE ENTIRE HISTORY OF THE WORLD TO THE 12th CENTURY

**THE NEW CHURCH of ADENSEN**
Germany, COMPLETED IN 1503,
USES THE BELFRY BUILT
FOR THE ORIGINAL CHURCH,
*ERECTED IN 1250*

## RENÉ ANTOINE de RÉAUMUR

THE FRENCH SCIENTIST,
DISCOVERED HOW TO
MAKE PAPER FROM
WOOD BY WATCHING
WASPS MAKE
PAPERLIKE NESTS BY
*CHEWING UP FOOD*

**NEW YORK'S GREAT FIRES**
OF 1835 AND 1845, RUINED MOST OF THE CITY'S
FIRE-INSURANCE COMPANIES--YET THE CLAIMS IN BOTH
FIRES *TOTALED LESS THAN $15,000,000*

**THE WINDMILL HOUSE**
Luneburger Heide, Germany,
A HOME IN THE SHAPE OF A
WINDMILL, BUILT AS A MEMORIAL
TO AN ANCIENT MILL *DESTROYED BY FIRE*

**THE ICE-CREAM CONE**
Phillip Island, Australia,
*NATURAL STONE FORMATION*

**THE WORST-DRESSED WOMEN IN THE WORLD**
A WOMAN OF THE TODA TRIBE OF SOUTHERN INDIA,
*GETS ONLY 2 GARMENTS THROUGHOUT HER ENTIRE LIFETIME*
SHE IS GIVEN ONE IN CHILDHOOD, AND THE SECOND WHEN SHE IS MARRIED

**ESKIMOS** OF THE TAIMYR PENINSULA, ARCTIC SIBERIA, USE THEIR SLEDS THROUGHOUT THE SUMMER THAW BECAUSE THE RUNNERS, MADE FOR SNOW, **WORK WELL ON THE MOSSY TUNDRA**

**COBY ORR** of San Antonio, Texas, PLAYING HIS FIRST ROUND OF GOLF, MADE A 103-YD. HOLE IN ONE *AT THE AGE OF 5*

**DEVIL'S TABLE** NEAR KALTENBACH, GERMANY--*NATURAL STONE FORMATION*

**DAVID J. COOK** (1840-1907) of Denver, Colorado, WAS A FARMER, GOLD MINER, SUPPLY-TRAIN OPERATOR, DETECTIVE, REAL-ESTATE OPERATOR, POLICE CHIEF, MARSHAL, SHERIFF AND MILITIA GENERAL-- *HE ARRESTED MORE THAN 3,000 MEN-- 50 OF THEM FOR MURDER*

**KING RICHARD I** of England, KNOWN AS RICHARD THE LION-HEARTED, RULED FOR A PERIOD OF 10 YEARS--BUT SPENT ONLY ABOUT 6 MONTHS OF HIS ENTIRE REIGN IN ENGLAND

THE **MERRY MAILBOX** A MAILBOX FITTED BY FRED MORGAN OF NORWOOD, N.Y., WITH A SOUSAPHONE THAT PLAYS TAPED MUSIC WHENEVER THE MAIL-BOX IS OPENED

Submitted by Jules Marr, Albuquerque, N.M.

THE **CHURCH OF SOMPTING** IS THE ONLY ONE IN ALL ENGLAND WITH A GABLED ROOF

**GOUVERNEUR MORRIS** (1752-1816) WHO HEADED THE COMMITTEE THAT WROTE THE FINAL DRAFT OF THE U.S. CONSTITUTION, HAD BEEN SUSPECTED OF SYMPATHIES FOR ENGLAND AT THE OUTBREAK OF THE AMERICAN REVOLUTION

**THE CHURCH OF SAMRODT**
POLAND.
ORIGINALLY, WAS A WING
*OF AN ANCIENT CASTLE*

**ROBERT BONNER**
WEALTHY OWNER OF A
NEW YORK NEWSPAPER,
HAD RELIGIOUS SCRUPLES
AGAINST ENTERING HIS FAMOUS
TROTTERS IN FORMAL RACES--
*BUT REGULARLY RACED THEM,
INFORMALLY, IN THE 1840'S,
AGAINST THOSE OF CORNELIUS
VANDERBILT ON THE CITY'S STREETS*

**DAVID GARRICK**
(1717-1779),
ENGLISH ACTOR AND
THEATRICAL MANAGER,
WAS THE FIRST
MANAGER TO DISCONTINUE
THE PRACTICE OF REDUCED
FEES TO PATRONS
WHO ARRIVED LATE--
*OR LEFT
EARLY*

**WARRIORS**
IN
ANCIENT
GAUL,
WORE A
HELMET OF
LEATHER
THAT
*PROTECTED
BOTH THEIR
HEAD AND
NECK*

THE **ST. CHARLES HOTEL** IN NEW ORLEANS, WAS DESTROYED BY FIRE IN 1851-- AS WAS A SECOND HOTEL OF THE SAME NAME, ON THE SAME LOCATION, *43 YEARS LATER*

**SHERWOOD ANDERSON** (1876-1941), THE FAMED AMERICAN WRITER, BOUGHT AND EDITED 2 RIVAL NEWSPAPERS IN MARION, VA., IN THE 1920's -- *ONE DEMOCRATIC AND THE OTHER REPUBLICAN*

**DR. PHILIP JAISOHN** (1860-1951), FOUNDER OF THE LIBERATION MOVEMENT IN KOREA, WAS THE FIRST WESTERN-TRAINED KOREAN GENERAL, THE FIRST AMERICAN- EDUCATED KOREAN DOCTOR, AND THE *FIRST KOREAN TO BECOME AN AMERICAN CITIZEN*

**ST. PAUL'S GATE** IN VERDUN, FRANCE, HAS A PLAQUE WHICH READS: "VERDUN, DESTROYED IN 10 MONTHS, FEB. TO DEC., 1916. REBUILT IN 10 YEARS, 1919-1929"

THE **FLOWER MANTIS**
(Hymenopus bicornis)
IN ITS PUPAL
STAGE, LIVES ON
A FLOWER --
INVISIBLE
BECAUSE ITS
WINGS AND WIDE
LEGS RESEMBLE
THE SURROUND-
ING PETALS

**THE FIRST OIL WELL**
SUNK IN TITUSVILLE, PA., IN
AUGUST, 1859, WAS INTENDED
ONLY TO INCREASE THE
SUPPLY OF "SENECA OIL"
*-- A PETROLEUM PATENT
MEDICINE PREVIOUSLY
GATHERED IN STREAMS*

**JAVANESE WOMEN**
DAILY SWEEP THEIR COFFEE
TREES WITH BROOMS

**MINERAL
CRYSTALS**
FORMING A
*NATURAL
SCULPTURE...*
Royal
Ontario
Museum,
Toronto, Ont.

THE **FIRST MALE CHAUVINIST** NICOLAS CHAUVIN, A FRENCH SOLDIER, WAS RESPONSIBLE FOR THE EXPRESSION "CHAUVINISM"-- WHICH MEANS FANATICAL PATRIOTISM. CHAUVIN WAS RIDICULED BY HIS FELLOW SOLDIERS FOR HIS EFFUSIVE PRAISE OF EMPEROR NAPOLEON, WHO, FOR A DISABLING WOUND, HAD GRANTED CHAUVIN A CEREMONIAL SABER, A RED RIBBON AND A PENSION OF $40 A YEAR

A **SINGLE AMERICAN OYSTER** LAYS 500,000,000 EGGS A YEAR--YET ONLY ONE OF THEM WILL NORMALLY REACH MATURITY

**HOW TO KEEP THE DENTIST AWAY**
A **SHARK'S TOOTH** IS WORN BY CHILDREN OF MALTA IN THE BELIEF THAT IT WILL ASSURE THEM *HEALTHY TEETH*

A **PUMPKIN**, DISPLAYED BY LORIE HELMER, of GREELEY, COLO., *THAT WEIGHS 198 POUNDS.*
Submitted by J.E. Kanost, Greeley, Colo.

**SPINES** of the SEA URCHIN, WHICH ARE ABOUT 6 INCHES LONG, ARE USED BY SCHOOL-CHILDREN OF RAROTONGA, IN THE PACIFIC, AS *SLATE PENCILS*

THE **MONARCH WHOSE VICTORY WAS FORETOLD BY A RIVAL!** KING EDWARD III of England, DEFEATED KING PHILIP VI, of France, AT CRÉCY, SLAYING 1,000 KNIGHTS AND 30,000 TROOPS, A VICTORY THAT HAD BEEN PREDICTED BY KING ROBERT, of Naples --*THE ONLY CROWNED HEAD OF EUROPE RECOGNIZED AS AN EXPERT ASTROLOGER*

A **STATUE** OF MAYOR JOSHUA GAGE OF BATTLE CREEK, MICH., *DEPICTS HIM AS A TRAMP...* GAGE DRESSED AS A TRAMP TO PROVE HIS SUSPICION THAT A TAVERN OWNER WAS SELLING LIQUOR ON SUNDAY --AND THE TAVERN OWNER COMMISSIONED THE ONE-TON STATUE AS HIS REVENGE

GO · SLOW
SLEEPING POLICEMAN
AHEAD

**SIGN** NEAR MONTEGO BAY, JAMAICA. Submitted by EMERY F. TOBIN, Vancouver, Wash.

The **TOSHOGU SHRINE**, Japan, BUILT AS A MAUSOLEUM FOR SHOGUN IEYASU, REQUIRED **3 YEARS** OF LABOR *BY 780,000 WORKERS*

## JOHN MERCER LANGSTON

(1829-1897), WHO WAS BORN A SLAVE, WAS ELECTED TOWN CLERK, IN LORAIN COUNTY, OHIO, IN 1855 —*THE FIRST BLACK AMERICAN TO HOLD AN ELECTIVE OFFICE*

**TRUGANINI** WHO DIED IN 1934, *WAS THE LAST TASMANIAN ABORIGINE*

**A BLUEGILL** CAUGHT BY RAY EMLEY, OF HUNTINGTON, IND., *HAD 2 MOUTHS.* Submitted by David Huffman, Markle, Ind.

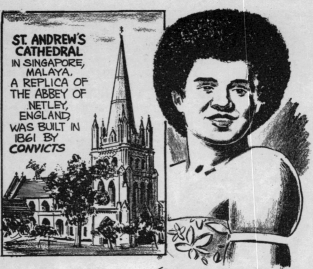

**ST. ANDREW'S CATHEDRAL** IN SINGAPORE, MALAYA, A REPLICA OF THE ABBEY OF NETLEY, ENGLAND, WAS BUILT IN 1861 BY **CONVICTS**

THE **FIRST WEIGHT WATCHERS PAPUAN GIRLS** IN NEW GUINEA, AFFIXED TIGHT METAL RINGS TO THEIR ARMS, WHICH MADE THE MUSCLES SWELL ON EITHER SIDE OF THE RINGS, *BECAUSE WIVES WERE BOUGHT BY THE POUND*

**OLIVER MOROSCO** THE BROADWAY PRODUCER, MADE MORE THAN $5,000,000 FROM A SUCCESSION OF HIT SHOWS--BUT WHEN HE DIED AT 69, HE HAD *8 CENTS IN HIS POCKET*

**A LOCK** INVENTED IN THE 1800'S, HELD SMALL EXPLOSIVE CAPS AND SURPRISED A BURGLAR *BY EXPLODING WITH A LOUD BANG*

## THE COIN THAT DELIVERED A MOST WELCOME MESSAGE

A COPPER COIN MINTED BY EMPEROR CALIGULA, OF ROME, IN 40 A.D., CARRIED A LATIN INSCRIPTION ANNOUNCING ABOLISHMENT OF AN INCOME TAX OF ½%

**THE WELL CHAPEL** IN DUPATH, ENGLAND, WAS BUILT BY A YOUNG MAN AS A PENANCE FOR *HAVING SLAIN A RIVAL FOR HIS SWEETHEART'S LOVE*

## SETTLERS

TO GET AROUND THE HOMESTEAD ACT OF 1862, WHICH PROVIDED THAT EACH CLAIM HAD TO HAVE A HOME MEASURING AT LEAST "12 X 12," OFTEN BUILT MINIATURE HOUSES *ONE FOOT HIGH AND ONE FOOT WIDE*

A **BICYCLE BED** BUILT BY JIM GLASS, of Riverside, Calif.

A **CANTALOUPE** 27 INCHES IN CIRCUMFERENCE AND WEIGHING 15 POUNDS- Grown by Mrs. W.W. Winters, Albuquerque, N.M.

THE ARCH OF VAUCOULEURS
France,
FORMERLY A GATE, IS THE
ONLY SURVIVING PART
OF AN ANCIENT CASTLE

THE REV. FREDERIC
HUIDEKOPER
(1817-1892), SERVED AT
THE THEOLOGICAL SCHOOL
IN MEADVILLE, PA.,
AS PROFESSOR OF
ECCLESIASTICAL HISTORY
AND NEW TESTAMENT
INTERPRETATION FOR
35 YEARS WITHOUT
COLLECTING A
CENT IN SALARY

Welcome to...
MARKLE
HOME OF 902 HAPPY PEOPLE
AND 4 GROUCHES

SIGN IN MARKLE, INDIANA.
Submitted by Kent Sommers,
Huntington, Ind.

THE OX-TEAM DRIVER, in Spain, WALKS AHEAD OF HIS TEAM--
HIS WHIP ALWAYS IN FULL VIEW OF THE OXEN

THE LEAD IN THE AVERAGE PENCIL WILL WRITE 45,000 WORDS OR DRAW A LINE 35 MILES LONG

SAILS ARE MADE BY YAP ISLANDERS BY INTERLACING LEAVES OF THE PANDANUS TREE

## CAPT. WILLIAM KIDD
(1645-1701),
BEFORE HE BECAME AN INFAMOUS PIRATE, *WAS RESPECTED AS A TRADER ON NEW YORK'S WALL STREET*

## FRANCIS HOPKINSON
(1737-1791), ONE OF THE SIGNERS OF THE DECLARATION OF INDEPENDENCE, *WAS AMERICA'S FIRST NATIVE COMPOSER.* HIS "MY DAYS HAVE BEEN SO WONDROUS FREE." IS THE FIRST PIECE OF MUSIC COMPOSED BY AN AMERICAN

**ROBERT FENTON** USING A PHOTOGRAPHIC VAN, MADE THE FIRST PICTORIAL RECORD OF WARFARE DURING THE CRIMEAN WAR-- *SEVERAL YEARS BEFORE MATTHEW BRADY PHOTOGRAPHED AMERICA'S CIVIL WAR*

**GALE KLAINE** OF WEST PALM BEACH, FLA., WAS BORN ON *FEBRUARY 8, 1957* -- HER FATHER WAS BORN *FEBRUARY 8, 1912* -- HER GRANDMOTHER WAS BORN *FEBRUARY 8, 1882*

**THE CROWLAND PARISH CHURCH** STILL USED FOR SERVICES IN CROWLAND, ENGLAND, ACTUALLY IS THE NORTH AISLE OF THE ABBEY CHURCH WHICH WAS BUILT 1,250 YEARS AGO, AND IS FOR THE MOST PART IN RUINS

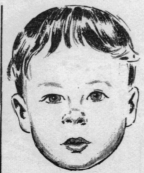

**ROBERT K. SCHULTZ** OF CHICAGO, ILL., WAS BORN AT 5:14 P.M., ON JUNE 14, 1974, IN THE 14th YEAR OF HIS PARENTS' MARRIAGE...

HIS MOTHER WAS BORN JUNE 14, 1937, AND HER MOTHER WAS BORN SEPT. 14, 1903

**AN OLD BARN**
NEAR LA HAMAIDE, BELGIUM, WHICH ONCE SERVED AS A HOUSE, HAS ALL ITS WINDOWS SEALED WITH WOODEN CROSSES.
*IT WAS LONG A CUSTOM TO SO SEAL UP THE HOME ON THE DAY ITS TENANT WAS BURIED*

**THE ILIMA** THE OFFICIAL FLOWER OF HAWAII, ONCE COULD BE WORN IN LEIS ONLY BY THE ISLAND CHIEFS

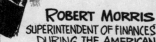

**ROBERT MORRIS** SUPERINTENDENT OF FINANCES DURING THE AMERICAN REVOLUTION, WAS PERMITTED TO CONDUCT PROFITABLE PRIVATE BUSINESS VENTURES WHILE SERVING THE GOVERNMENT BECAUSE *NO ONE ELSE IN THE COUNTRY COULD HANDLE HIS JOB*

**THE MARQUIS de LAFAYETTE** - (1757-1834) - HERO OF THE AMERICAN REVOLUTION, JOINED THE FRENCH ARMY IN 1771, BUT WAS FORCED TO RETIRE 5 YEARS LATER--*AT THE AGE OF 18*

**THE "JOYITA"** A 70-TON VESSEL THAT SAILED FROM APIA, WESTERN SAMOA, FOR THE TOKELAU ISLANDS ON OCT. 3, 1955, WITH 25 PERSONS ABOARD, WAS FOUND ADRIFT 37 DAYS LATER -- *WITH NO INDICATION OF THE FATE OF HER PASSENGERS AND CREW*

ANTOINE LAVOISIER (1743-1794), THE FRENCH CHEMIST, WAS A REVOLUTIONARY AND URGED SUCH REFORMS AS TAXES ON THE NOBILITY AND A FREE PRESS *--YET BECAUSE HE HAD BEEN A LANDOWNER AND COLLECTED TAXES, HE WAS GUILLOTINED IN THE FRENCH REVOLUTION*

A **CHINESE CALENDAR** ENGRAVED IN THE 16th CENTURY *ON THE SHOULDER-BLADE OF AN OX*

THE **CAVEMAN** NEAR RUHLA, GERMANY, *NATURAL ROCK FORMATION*

THE **PICKPOCKET WHO BECAME A POLICE CHIEF**
GEORGE BARRINGTON, A NOTORIOUS ENGLISH PICKPOCKET, WHO WAS DEPORTED TO AUSTRALIA FOR HIS THEFTS, BECAME *POLICE CHIEF OF PARRAMATTA, AUSTRALIA*

**ADRIENNE COUVREUR** OF NEUVILLE, ST. VAAST, FRANCE, AT THE AGE OF 90, WITNESSED THE INVASION OF FRANCE BY GERMANY *FOR THE THIRD TIME*

**WILLIAM THE CONQUEROR** (1027-1087) FATHERED THE MODERN JURY SYSTEM BY SETTING UP JURIES OF 12 MEN IN EACH DISTRICT, TO ASSURE *HONEST TAX PAYMENTS*

A **GRAVE MARKER** IN THE OLD CEMETERY OF SAN PEDRO, QUESTA, N.M., IS A TREE TRUNK IN THE SHAPE OF A CROSS

A **KEY** MADE IN ITALY DURING THE RENAISSANCE PERIOD, FEATURING A HEART AND TWO FIGURES, *GUARDED THE CONTENTS OF A MARRIAGE CHEST*

AN **ICE-CREAM SUNDAE** MADE BY ROBERT BERCAW, of Wooster, Ohio, WAS 14 FEET HIGH, WEIGHED 3,514 POUNDS AND CONTAINED *50 FLAVORS OF ICE CREAM.* – May 9, 1975 –

Submitted by Jules H. Marr, Albuquerque, N.M.

THE MASDE-VALLIA SIMULA ORCHID IS CALLED *PARTRIDGE IN THE GRASS*

THE CHURCH of NOTRE DAME du PORT IN CLERMONT-FERRAND, FRANCE, HAD ITS BELFRIES RAZED DURING THE FRENCH REVOLUTION -- *SO THE STRUCTURE WOULD CONFORM TO THE REVOLUTIONARY IDEA OF EQUALITY*

THE WASHINGTON MONUMENT in Washington, D.C., ON WHICH ALL WORK WAS HALTED FOR A PERIOD OF 20 YEARS, WAS DESCRIBED BY MARK TWAIN IN 1873 AS LOOKING LIKE *" A FACTORY CHIMNEY WITH THE TOP BROKEN OFF "*

AN UMBRELLA DESIGNED WITH A HOLLOW HANDLE *IN WHICH TO CARRY CIGARS*

**THE SOUTH HEAD LIGHTHOUSE** in Australia, WAS CONSTRUCTED BY A CONVICT-ARCHITECT--*WHO WAS PARDONED FOR HIS WORK*

A **FIRE-WALKING CEREMONY** IS HELD FREQUENTLY IN SAN PEDRO, SPAIN, WITH MOST OF THE POPULATION *WALKING BAREFOOT THROUGH RED-HOT COALS.* AN ILL RESIDENT OFTEN IS CARRIED ON A FRIEND'S BACK

FACTS ABOUT GEORGIA

A **BOOK** CONTAINING FACTS ABOUT THE STATE OF GEORGIA WAS PUBLISHED. IN 1916, IN *THE SHAPE OF THE STATE'S BOUNDARIES*

**Johan Cesare Godeffroy** of Hamburg, Germany, IS THE 7th CONSECUTIVE MEMBER OF HIS FAMILY *TO BEAR THAT NAME*

**AN OCCUPIED HOME**
in Belingries, Germany, LOCATED ON A TOWER *OF THE TOWN WALL*

**A MOHAMMEDAN MINARET** ON PEMBA ISLAND, NEAR ZANZIBAR, THAT WAS CLIMBED REGULARLY AT PRAYER TIMES, HAD TO BE ABANDONED WHEN BEES *BUILT A NEST BENEATH ITS ROOF*

**THE STRANGEST PILGRIMAGES IN THE WORLD!** **SHIA MOHAMMEDANS** ANNUALLY JOURNEY FROM THE HEADWATERS OF THE EUPHRATES RIVER, IN MESOPOTAMIA, TO THE HOLY CITY OF KERBELA, IRAQ, *FLOATING 800 MILES, FOR DAYS AND NIGHTS, NAKED AND CLINGING TO A WATERPROOF BAG OF ANIMAL SKINS CONTAINING THEIR CLOTHING AND FOOD*

DANVILLE, KY.
JUN 8
1975

Mr. Ed. Mattson
10906 Florian av.
Cleveland Ohio
44111

## A LETTER

MAILED BY SHARON KAY OSTER OF DANVILLE, KY., TO EDWARD MATTSON, OF CLEVELAND, OHIO, WAS CANCELLED AND DELIVERED ALTHOUGH *THE ENVELOPE HAD A DIME TAPED WHERE A STAMP SHOULD HAVE BEEN AFFIXED*

Submitted by Ralph B. Williams, Juneau, Alaska

"CORRIE" A SCOTTISH TERRIER, 15 INCHES LONG, WHILE PLAYING WITH HER OWNER, MRS. AUDREY MACASKILL, IN CHORLTON-CUM-HARDY, MANCHESTER, ENGLAND, *SWALLOWED A KNITTING NEEDLE 12 INCHES LONG --*

Submitted by Tom Harrison, Northwich, Cheshire, England

## A MANOR HOUSE

70 FEET LONG AND 50 FEET WIDE, BUILT IN LEXINGTON, KY., IN 1812, *IN EXCHANGE FOR 2 MERINO SHEEP*

## THE TOWER OF CONSTANCE

IN AIGUES MORTES, FRANCE, *HAS WALLS 23 FEET THICK*

94

THE **AUTOMOBILE ROAD** LEADING TO THE PEAK OF PICACHO DE VELETA, SPAIN, REACHES AN ALTITUDE OF 11,450 FEET--*THE HIGHEST AUTO HIGHWAY IN EUROPE*

A **FERTILITY SHRINE** in Japan, IS PILED WITH ROCKS BY MOTHERS WHO, IN GRATITUDE FOR ITS HELP, EACH ADD A STONE ON WHICH THEY HAVE WRITTEN THE SEX AND BIRTHDAY OF THEIR BABY

THE **"OLD MAN"** A DOLL HONORED AT THE HARVEST DANCE IN POMERANIA, POLAND, IS ALWAYS MADE FROM THE LAST SHEAF OF WHEAT HARVESTED

THE **HORNED LARK** of North America, HAS 2 TUFTS OF FEATHERS ATOP ITS HEAD THAT RESEMBLE HORNS

THE **COUNCIL APOTHECARY** IN GOTTINGER, GERMANY, HAS BEEN OPERATING IN THE SAME BUILDING *FOR 422 YEARS*

THE **BLISTER BUSH** FOUND ON THE CAPE PENINSULA, So. Africa, WHEN TOUCHED, CAUSES LARGE, PAINFUL BLISTERS

**CHARLES LAMB**
(1775-1834),
ENGLISH AUTHOR AND ESSAYIST, NEVER MARRIED BECAUSE HE WAS MADE LIFETIME GUARDIAN OF HIS SISTER, MARY, *--WHO HAD KILLED THEIR MOTHER*

THE **LINKED BIRCHES** near Mt. Vernon, Wash., *2 TREES JOINED BY AN ARCHED TRUNK* Submitted by Emery F. Tobin, Vancouver

**THE GUINEA**
A BAR IN LONDON, ENGLAND, HAS BEEN DOING BUSINESS ON THE SAME SPOT **FOR 553 YEARS**

A **39-STORY HOUSE OF CARDS** CREATED BY JOHN WILSON, OF PORT CREDIT, ONT., *USING 1,240 PLAYING CARDS*

**THE MEERKAT** of So. Africa, APPEARS TO HAVE A SEAM FROM THE MIDDLE OF ITS CHIN DOWN THE ENTIRE LENGTH OF ITS BODY... *MAKING IT LOOK LIKE A STUFFED ANIMAL*

**ABRAHAM VERHOEVEN** WAS THE FIRST BELGIAN NEWSPAPERMAN-- FOUNDING A PAPER CALLED "NEW TIDINGS," THAT WAS PUBLISHED FROM 1605 UNTIL 1827

*THE* **RÖK-STONE** of Sweden, HAS THE LARGEST QUANTITY OF ANCIENT RUNIC INSCRIPTIONS FOUND ANYWHERE IN THE WORLD

**A NATURAL SAUNA**
ON THE BEACH AT BEPPU, KYUSHU ISLAND, JAPAN, CREATED BY STEAM FROM AN UNDERGROUND VOLCANO THAT HEATS THE SAND WITH WHICH MEN AND WOMEN COVER THEMSELVES

**ROCK FORMATION**
ON MOUNT SERBAL,
IN THE SINAI DESERT,
SHAPED LIKE THE
*SKULL OF AN OX*

**JOHN P. MORGAN**
(1837-1913), THE FINANCIER,
DURING THE FINANCIAL CRISIS
OF 1907 SIGNED A NOTE ON
HIS PERSONAL STATIONERY
*PLEDGING TO SUPPORT THE
CREDIT OF NEW YORK CITY
BY PURCHASE OF $30,000,000
OF THE CITY'S REVENUE BONDS*

**FISHER AMES**
(1758-1808) AMERICAN
STATESMAN AND
POLITICAL ESSAYIST,
ENTERED HARVARD
UNIVERSITY AT **12**,
*AND WAS GRADUATED
AT 16*

**PIRATE'S FACE**
NATURAL FORMATION IN A
TREE TRUNK IN INTERLOCHEN
STATE PARK, INTERLOCHEN, MICH.
*Submitted by* CHRISTOPHER
POWERS, Grand Rapids, Mich.,
and BILL LUYK, Marne, Mich.

THE **PINE TREE SHILLING** A SILVER COIN ISSUED BY THE FIRST COLONIAL MINT, WAS REISSUED FOR A PERIOD OF **30 YEARS--** BUT THE 1652 DATE WAS NEVER CHANGED

THE **DANCING ATTIRE** OF NATIVES OF THE PUAMO ISLANDS, IN THE EASTERN PACIFIC, IS A SHOULDER AND ANKLE COVERING MADE *FROM THE HAIR OF DEPARTED ANCESTORS*

THE **REV. JOHN SCRIPPS** (1785-1865), A METHODIST PREACHER, IN VIRGINIA, FOR 52 YEARS, READ THE BIBLE EVERY DAY OF HIS LIFE FOR **72** YEARS, *READING IT FROM COVER TO COVER* **2,600 TIMES**

**BRANDS** AFFIXED TO LOGS IN THE U.S. NORTHWEST BEFORE BEING FLOATED DOWN-RIVER SO THEY COULD BE ROUNDED UP BY THE PROPER SAWMILL

**THE BRIDGE** OVER THE COAL RIVER AT RICHMOND, TASMANIA, BUILT IN 1823, IS THE OLDEST SPAN IN AUSTRALIA

**GABY DESLYS** THE FRENCH ACTRESS, STARRED IN A REVUE ORIGINALLY NAMED "Saucy Suzette," BUT THE TITLE WAS SHORTENED BECAUSE "SAUCY" WAS CONSIDERED VULGAR IN THE EARLY 1900's

**TED MORFORD** OF NEWPORT BEACH, CALIF., WEARS A LAPEL PIN DISPLAYING 2 PEARLS HE FOUND IN A *BOWL OF OYSTER STEW*

THE **RHAETIAN RAILWAY** OF SWITZERLAND, IN 245 MILES, TRAVERSES *488 BRIDGES AND 119 TUNNELS*

**NED KELLY** AN AUSTRALIAN HIGHWAYMAN WHO WAS EXECUTED IN 1880, ALWAYS WORE A COAT OF ARMOR *BEATEN OUT OF PLOUGH-SHARES*

A **CAKE** BAKED IN COLOGNE, GERMANY, FOR GIRLS CONSIDERED SOCIAL CLIMBERS, IS SHAPED LIKE A *CHIMNEY-SWEEP*

THE **OLDEST THEATER TICKETS** ARE CIRCULAR MARKERS ISSUED FREE BY ANCIENT GREECE-- *EACH BEARING A LETTER TO INDICATE THE SEAT RESERVED*

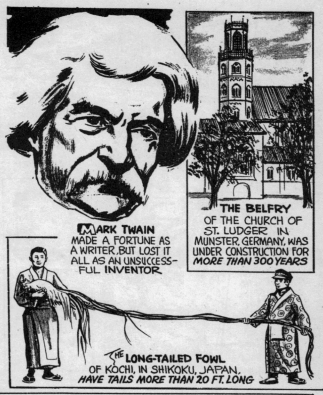

**MARK TWAIN** MADE A FORTUNE AS A WRITER, BUT LOST IT ALL AS AN UNSUCCESSFUL **INVENTOR**

**THE BELFRY** OF THE CHURCH OF ST. LUDGER IN MUNSTER, GERMANY, WAS UNDER CONSTRUCTION FOR *MORE THAN 300 YEARS*

THE **LONG-TAILED FOWL** OF KOCHI, IN SHIKOKU, JAPAN, *HAVE TAILS MORE THAN 20 FT. LONG*

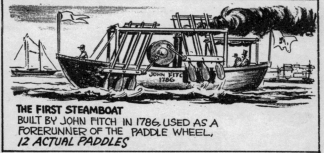

**THE FIRST STEAMBOAT** BUILT BY JOHN FITCH IN 1786, USED AS A FORERUNNER OF THE PADDLE WHEEL, *12 ACTUAL PADDLES*

JOHN FITCH 1786

**BANK'S ARCADE** IN NEW ORLEANS, A 3-STORY, BLOCK-LONG STRUCTURE, WAS THE PRIZE IN AN 1839 LOTTERY

**GERONIMO** THE APACHE INDIAN WHO TERRORIZED THE SOUTHWEST DURING THE 1880's, ENDED HIS DAYS SELLING HIS PHOTOGRAPHS FOR 25 CENTS EACH

**FEMALE TICKS** LAY AS MANY AS 5,000 EGGS AT A TIME

**LOOKING GLASS ROCK** Pisgah National Forest, N.C., IN WET WEATHER IT GLISTENS LIKE A GIANT MIRROR

**WILLIAM PENN** (1644-1718)
THE QUAKER WHO FOUNDED PENNSYLVANIA,
SUGGESTED FORMATION OF A UNITED
NATIONS ORGANIZATION **283 YEARS AGO**

**MONTICELLO**
THE VIRGINIA HOME
OF THOMAS
JEFFERSON, HAS
ONLY 2 EXTREMELY
NARROW STAIR-
WAYS BECAUSE
*JEFFERSON CON-
SIDERED THEM A
WASTE OF SPACE*

**THE SHIELD**
CARRIED BY CHIEF
ARAPOOSH OF THE
CROW INDIANS OF
MONTANA, WAS CON-
SIDERED A MAGICAL
REPRESENTATION OF
THE MOON, AND WAS
*SPUN TO DECIDE
TRIBAL PROBLEMS*

**THE ELGIN BOTANICAL GARDEN**
IN NEW YORK CITY, BOUGHT
BY DR. DAVID HOSACK IN 1801
FOR **$5,000**, IS NOW THE SITE OF
*ROCKEFELLER CENTER*

**THE CHURCH OF DENSUS**
RUMANIA,
WAS BUILT ON THE RUINS OF
AN ANCIENT ROMAN WALL

*THE* **WORLD'S SMALLEST TROPHY**
*A SOLID GOLD LOVING CUP*
PRESENTED TO R. MAX RITTER
WHEN HE WAS PRESIDENT
OF THE INTERNATIONAL
GOVERNING BODY OF SWIMMING,
AND DISPLAYED IN THE SWIMMING
HALL OF FAME, FORT LAUDER-
DALE, FLA., WAS MADE FROM A
THIMBLE AND A COLLAR BUTTON,
**AND IS ONLY ONE INCH HIGH**

**FILIBUSTER**
MEANING THE
TACTIC TO
OBSTRUCT
PASSAGE
OF A BILL, COMES
FROM THE
FRENCH WORD
"FLIBUSTIER"
*--MEANING A*
*FREEBOOTER*
*OR PIRATE*

**"AUDLEY END"**
THE HOME OF THOMAS HOWARD, LORD HIGH TREASURER OF
ENGLAND, WAS DESCRIBED BY KING JAMES I AS
*"TOO LARGE FOR A KING -- THOUGH IT MIGHT DO*
*FOR A LORD TREASURER."*
HOWARD WAS SUBSE- QUENTLY CHARGED WITH
MISAPPROPRIATING PUBLIC FUNDS

## LORD CORNWALLIS

( 1738-1805 )

REMEMBERED BEST BY AMERICANS FOR HIS DEFEAT AT YORKTOWN, OPPOSED BRITAIN'S POLICY OF TAXING THE COLONIES-- *A STAND THAT HAD FORCED HIM TO WITHDRAW FROM THE HOUSE OF LORDS*

## A CLAY PIPE

MADE IN MEXICO, IN THE SHAPE OF A YOUNG WOMAN-- *ONE FOOT IS THE MOUTHPIECE, AND THE BOWL IS LOCATED BETWEEN HER SHOULDERS*

## OIL

WHEN IT WAS FIRST DISCOVERED AT SPINDLETOP, TEXAS, IN 1901, SOLD FOR 3¢ A BARREL--COMPARED TO THE GOING PRICE FOR WATER THERE AT **$6** A BARREL

## CATHARINE BEECHER

(1800-1878), FEMINIST AND EARLY SUPPORTER OF EDUCATION FOR WOMEN, BELIEVED THAT EDUCATION SHOULD PREPARE WOMEN ONLY FOR THEIR "TRUE PROFESSION" --HOME-MAKING

**DEATH NOTICES** IN NEW ORLEANS, IN THE 1890'S, WERE *TACKED ON BUILDINGS OR LAMPPOSTS*

THE **OLD GRAND CENTRAL STATION** IN NEW YORK CITY, WAS KEPT CLEAN OF SMOKE AND SOOT BY A STRICTLY ENFORCED RULE THAT PASSENGER TRAINS HAD TO BE *COASTED IN--WITHOUT ENGINES*

**FANS** FOUND IN THE TOMB OF PHARAOH TUTANKHAMEN, STILL HAD SOME OF THEIR OSTRICH FEATHERS INTACT AFTER MORE *THAN 3,000 YEARS*

THE **REV. DANIEL WALDO** (1762-1864), of Syracuse, N.Y., A VETERAN OF THE REVOLUTIONARY WAR, WAS A MINISTER FOR 72 YEARS

**THE ANGEL'S TRUMPET**
A TROPICAL FLOWER,
NAMED FOR ITS WHITE
TRUMPET-SHAPED FLOWERS

A **PAMPHLET**
ENTITLED:
"NEW YORK
CITY'S
PROGRESS
TOWARD
BANKRUPTCY"
WAS PUBLISHED
BY EDGAR J.
LEVEY, A
FORMER OFFICIAL
IN THE CITY'S
COMPTROLLER'S
OFFICE,
IN 1908!

Sir **FREDERICK BANTING** (1891-1941),
THE CANADIAN PHYSICIAN WHO
DISCOVERED INSULIN, HAD WORKED ON
THE PROBLEM ONLY 8 MONTHS

THE **CHURCH OF PELLWORM**
Germany,
BUILT IN 1362,
MAKES USE OF THE
BELFRY OF A CHURCH
*CONSTRUCTED IN 1095*

THE **TOWERING
HILLS**
BUILT BY
MAGNETIC ANTS
--SO NAMED
BECAUSE THEIR
SKYSCRAPER
NESTS ALWAYS
POINT NORTH
AND SOUTH,
*ARE FOUND
ONLY IN
NORTHERN
AUSTRALIA*

THE **PARSON CAPEN HOUSE** STILL STANDING IN TOPSFIELD, MASS., WAS *BUILT IN 1684*

THE **PARADISE FISH** OF THAILAND, BUILDS ITS NEST UNDERWATER, BRINGING AIR FROM THE SURFACE, AND SALIVA TO CREATE *A NEST OF BUBBLES*

**HENRY CLAY** (1777-1852), HAILED BY HISTORIANS AS ONE OF KENTUCKY'S MOST FAMOUS SONS, *ACTUALLY WAS BORN AND REARED IN VIRGINIA*

4-8

THE **CHURCH OF DAMME**, Belgium, ON WHICH CONSTRUCTION WAS STARTED WHEN THE TOWN ENJOYED A BRIEF BOOM, HAS *BEEN LEFT UNFINISHED FOR MORE THAN A CENTURY*

ROCKS on Fosheim Peninsula, Ellesmere Isl., in the Arctic, SUBJECTED TO EXTREME HEAT AND COLD, SHATTER INTO STRANGE SHAPES

HORACE MANN (1796-1859) FAMED AS AN AMERICAN EDUCATOR, WAS A FIRM BELIEVER IN *PHRENOLOGY--JUDGING CHARACTER BY THE SHAPE OF THE SKULL*

A **$55 NOTE** ISSUED IN THE U.S. IN 1779

**DOROTHEA DIX** AS SUPERINTENDENT OF NURSES IN THE CIVIL WAR, REFUSED TO EMPLOY ANY NURSE *WHO WAS NOT HOMELY*

THE CHURCH OF COUTARD
France, BUILT IN THE 11th CENTURY,
HAS BEEN USED SINCE THE
FRENCH REVOLUTION AS A BARN

STEPHEN A. DOUGLAS
ALTHOUGH HE LOST
A SWEETHEART,
MARY TODD, AND
THE PRESIDENCY
TO ABRAHAM LINCOLN,
GRACIOUSLY
*WROTE A LETTER
OF INTRODUCTION
TO HARVARD
UNIVERSITY
FOR LINCOLN'S
SON, ROBERT*

THE WREN BUILDING
AT THE COLLEGE OF WILLIAM AND MARY IN WILLIAMSBURG VA.,
ERECTED IN 1695, *IS THE OLDEST ACADEMIC BUILDING IN
AMERICA STILL IN USE*

**THE OLD U.S. MINT** IN NEW ORLEANS, LA., WAS THE ONLY MINT EVER USED FOR A FANCY DRESS BALL-- IT WAS HELD IN 1850 TO HONOR ROSE AND JOSEPHINE KENNEDY, DAUGHTERS OF THE MINT'S SUPERINTENDENT

THE **ALPHABET TREE**
A TREE IN Shamchruorasi, India, WITH ENGLISH LETTERS *FORMED BY NATURE ON THE BARK*
Submitted by Harjindar Singh Kalsi, Parkfield, Wolverhampton, England

THE **PARISH CHURCH** of Dettelbach, Germany, HAS TWIN BELFRIES --*LINKED BY AN ENCLOSED BRIDGE*

**GENERAL GAISHI NAGAOKA**
THE FATHER OF JAPAN'S AIR FORCE, HAD A MUSTACHE 20 INCHES LONG, AND UPON HIS DEATH IN 1933 *IT WAS BURIED WITH FULL HONORS IN A SEPARATE CASKET*

**A WATER WHEEL**
NEAR OCHOS RIOS, JAMAICA,
*ENCIRCLED BY A TREE*
Submitted by Adam and Eric
Frehm, No. Syracuse, N.Y.

A **HUGE WHITE LANTERN**
IS OFTEN CARRIED IN
CHINESE FUNERALS INSCRIBED
WITH THE DECEASED'S NAME AND
GOOD DEEDS-- *AND WITH YEARS
ADDED TO HIS AGE TO ADD
TO HIS IMPORTANCE*

**MARY CATHERINE HELLEN**
WHO BECAME
MRS. JOHN ADAMS II
IN 1828
WAS THE
ONLY BRIDE
MARRIED
IN THE
WHITE HOUSE
*TO THE SON OF A
U.S. PRESIDENT*

MRS. DOLORES P. WATERS of Walden, N.Y., RECOVERED A HIGH SCHOOL RING THAT HAD BEEN LOST ON THE BEACH AT ATLANTIC CITY, N.J., *25 YEARS BEFORE!* WHEN IT WAS RETURNED TO MRS. WATERS IT FIT ONLY THE FINGER OF HER DAUGHTER, RENEE

THE **TOWN HALL** OF SOMERS, N.Y., ORIGINALLY WAS THE ELEPHANT HOTEL -- BUILT BENEATH A TOWERING STATUE OF "OLD BET," *THE FIRST ELEPHANT FEATURED IN A TOURING CIRCUS*

ANDREW JACKSON AT THE AGE OF 78 BECAME THE FIRST U.S. PRESIDENT *TO HAVE HIS PICTURE TAKEN*

**GEORGES GUYNEMER**
WHO BECAME A PILOT IN THE FRENCH AIR FORCE IN WORLD WAR I, AFTER HAVING FIRST BEEN REJECTED FOR POOR HEALTH, SHOT DOWN 53 ENEMY AIRCRAFT AND SURVIVED BEING SHOT DOWN HIMSELF 8 TIMES

THE **BELFRY** OF THE CHURCH OF KIPPEN, SCOTLAND, IS THE ONLY PART OF THE STRUCTURE STILL STANDING — COVERED WITH CENTURIES OF IVY

A **RELIC** PRESERVED IN THE CATHEDRAL OF ST. BLASIUS, in Ragusa, Yugoslavia, *IS THE JAW OF ST. STEPHEN, ONCE THE KING OF HUNGARY*

THE **ALBATROSS** HAS A HOOKED BEAK WITH WHICH IT CAN EXERT AS MUCH FORCE *AS A PICKAXE*

THE **WIREWORM** THE GRUB OF THE CLICK BEETLE LOOKS LIKE *A PIECE OF WIRE*

THE **MODERN BRIDGE OF ST. CONO** OVER THE PLATANO RIVER IN BUCCINO, ITALY, STANDS BESIDE AN ANCIENT ROMAN SPAN BUILT **2,000** YEARS AGO

**SKIS** CALLED NORWEGIAN SNOWSHOES IN THE U.S. IN 1897, *WERE USUALLY 14 FEET LONG*

**JERZY KOSINSKI** THE POLISH-BORN WRITER WHO LEARNED ENGLISH AS AN ADULT IN NEW YORK CITY, REVEALED THAT HE OBTAINED GUIDANCE IN GRAMMAR AND SYNTAX HUNDREDS OF TIMES BY DIALING THE *TELEPHONE OPERATOR*

**HENRY HOBSON RICHARDSON**
ARCHITECT FOR SUCH NOTED STRUCTURES AS BOSTON'S TRINITY CHURCH, WAS SO INTRIGUED BY MEDIEVAL THINGS THAT *IN HIS HOME HE OFTEN WORE THE ROBES OF A MONK*

THE *MEMORIAL* IN MOUX, FRANCE, TO FRENCH AUTHOR HENRI BATAILLE, (1872-1922), *SHOWS HIM AS A SKELE-TONIZED FIGURE*

**WEALTHY WOMEN**
IN 17th CENTURY RUSSIA, WORE PEARL-STUDDED HATS TO HIDE THEIR PATES-- *WHICH WERE SHAVED AT THEIR MARITAL CEREMONY*

A *SINGLE DROP OF WATER* CONTAINS *100 BILLION, BILLION ATOMS*

## PIERRE JACOTOT
### (1756-1821)

A PROFESSOR AT THE LYCEUM OF DIJON, FRANCE, HAVING BEEN LEFT PENNILESS BY NAPOLEON'S OUSTER, WAS BEQUEATHED AN INCOME EQUIVALENT TO $120,000 A YEAR BY A *FORMER PUPIL HE HAD GIVEN A FAILING GRADE*

**HOMES** OF THE CATALONIANS OF SPAIN, HAVE PALM BRANCHES AFFIXED TO THEM IN THE BELIEF *IT WILL PROTECT THEM FROM LIGHTNING*

**THE CATHEDRAL** NEAR KIAMA, NEW SO. WALES, *NATURAL ROCK FORMATION*

THE **ROYAL POINCIANA** A TROPICAL TREE, PRODUCES ITS FLOWERS *BEFORE IT BEARS LEAVES*

3-8

**DEWITT CLINTON** AS MAYOR OF NEW YORK CITY, IN 1814, WHEN THE BRITISH HAD BURNED THE CAPITOL AND WHITE HOUSE IN WASHINGTON, D.C., ARRANGED TO LOAN THE GOVERNMENT OF THE UNITED STATES $1,000,000

**RICHARD L. McFADDEN** of Lansing, Mich., HAS COLLECTED TEARSHEETS OF Believe It or Not CARTOONS SINCE 1938— *FILLING 42 SCRAPBOOKS*

**Amelia Jenks BLOOMER** (1818-1894), THE FEMINIST, IN 1849 FOUNDED "THE LILY" --*THE FIRST AMERICAN PUBLICATION EDITED BY, AND FOR, WOMEN*

A **BED WRENCH** WAS A NECESSITY IN COLONIAL AMERICA, BECAUSE IN THE DAYS BEFORE SPRINGS A ROPE WAS LACED ACROSS THE FRAME OF THE BED, AND *THE WRENCH TOOK UP THE SAG*

**SALISBURY CATHEDRAL** IN Salisbury, England, ORIGINALLY STOOD IN OLD SARUM, BUT WAS TAKEN DOWN AND REBUILT ON ITS PRESENT SITE-- *A TASK THAT REQUIRED 40 YEARS*

**IT PAYS TO HAVE A BIG MOUTH** THE PADDLEFISH, FOUND IN THE GREAT LAKES AND MISSISSIPPI RIVER SYSTEM, CATCHES FOOD MERELY BY *SWIMMING ALONG WITH ITS MOUTH OPEN*

**AN ANGUS COW** OWNED BY EARL PETERSON OF DECATUR, ARK., GAVE BIRTH TO *QUADRUPLET CALVES* (June 4, 1975)

THE LEANING TOWER
OF DAUSENAU, Germany,
A TILTING TOWER OF
THE OLD TOWN WALL

WINSTON CHURCHILL
WHO ESCAPED FROM A PRISONER
OF WAR CAMP IN THE BOER
WAR IN 1899, WAS HUNTED
BY THE POSTING OF
A 25-POUND REWARD
FOR HIS CAPTURE--
*DEAD OR ALIVE*

THE **RAINBOW CAKE**
BAKED
ANNUALLY IN
GERMANY
SINCE
ANCIENT TIMES
TO CELEBRATE
THE DAWNING
OF EACH
NEW YEAR

THE **RUNE STONE**
at Jelling, Denmark,
SET UP BY KING
HARALD THE
BLUETOOTH IN THE
10th CENTURY,
*BEARS THE FIRST
MENTION OF THE
NAME OF DENMARK*

**THE POTTERY MARK** ON THE WARES OF PIANTA PEDIS, WHOSE NAME IN LATIN MEANS "THE SOLE OF THE FOOT," WAS THIS IMPRESSION OF A SOLE--FOUND AT Hallstatt, Austria, 1900 **YEARS AGO**

**GEORGE HALLOCK** (1834-1917), ONETIME EDITOR OF THE NEW HAVEN, CONN., REGISTER, LIVED TO THE AGE OF **83** *AFTER SURVIVING 28 NARROW ESCAPES FROM DEATH*

**CORAL ROCK** SHAPED LIKE A *NUCLEAR EXPLOSION*-- IN A LAGOON ON PEMBA ISLAND NEAR ZANZIBAR

**JEAN de HOUSSAY** (1539-1609), A FRENCH MONK, ATE ONLY ONE MEAL A DAY FOR **48** YEARS, BREAD, WATER AND A FEW RAW ROOTS

THE **SHOES** WORN BY AUSTRALIAN ABORIGINES HAVE SOLES MADE OF WHITE EMU FEATHERS *WHICH LEAVE NO TRACKS INDICATING DIRECTION*

## THE OLD SOLDIER

ANDREAS TSCHURTSCHENBACHER WON THE GOLD MEDAL OF VALOR AS A SERGEANT IN AUSTRIA'S WAR AGAINST ITALY, IN 1866, AND THEN ENLISTED AGAIN TO FIGHT IN WORLD WAR I *AT THE AGE OF 70*

POST WINDMILLS, USED IN COLONIAL AMERICA, WERE MOUNTED ON A POST THAT SERVED AS A TURNTABLE SO *THEIR SAILS COULD BE FACED INTO THE PREVAILING WIND*

THE **RED-CAPPED MANGABEY** of Africa, COMMUNICATES WITH OTHER MONKEYS OF THE SAME BREED *BY BLINKING ITS WHITE EYELIDS LIKE SEMAPHORES*

**RONDO HATTON**
(1894-1946) AN AMERICAN ACTOR, PLAYED A MONSTER IN HORROR FILMS **WITHOUT MAKE-UP**

*THE LEANING MINARET*
ON THE MOSQUE OF SIWA, EGYPT, **IS 3 FEET OFF CENTER**

**GIRLS**
ATTENDING THE RUSSIAN STATE SMOLNY INSTITUTE, IN THE EARLY 20th CENTURY, WERE KEPT IN SECLUSION FOR A PERIOD OF **7** YEARS-- *DENIED PERMISSION TO SEE EVEN THEIR OWN FAMILIES*

HASSAN ARFA of Iran, WAS APPOINTED TO THE HIGHEST OFFICE, BELOW THAT OF EMPEROR, AT THE AGE OF 4 -- BECAUSE HE TOLD THE RULER HE WOULD LOOK BETTER IF HE DYED HIS GRAY MUSTACHE

THE **FIRST FLAG** OF THE CONFEDERACY WAS CHANGED AFTER ITS STARS AND BARS WERE MISTAKEN FOR THE UNION BANNER, *AND FIRED UPON BY REBEL TROOPS*

**FATHER WILLIAM MATTHEWS** (1770-1854), OF WASHINGTON, D.C., IN 1800 BECAME THE FIRST NATIVE AMERICAN ORDAINED AS A CATHOLIC PRIEST ON AMERICAN SOIL-- HIS 6 UNCLES WERE PRIESTS AND HIS AUNT AND 2 SISTERS WERE NUNS

**THE FIRST U.S. TREASURY** A SMALL IRON CHEST KEPT BY ROBERT MORRIS, GEORGE WASHINGTON'S SUPT. OF FINANCES, *HELD ALL THE HARD MONEY THAT FINANCED THE AMERICAN REVOLUTION*

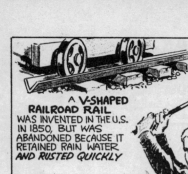

**A V-SHAPED RAILROAD RAIL** WAS INVENTED IN THE U.S. IN 1850, BUT WAS ABANDONED BECAUSE IT RETAINED RAIN WATER *AND RUSTED QUICKLY*

THE **MOST AMAZING ROUND OF GOLF IN THE GAME'S HISTORY** *Ray Fiore* of River Vale, N.Y., PLAYING IN A GOLF TOURNAMENT AT CASTLE HARBOR, BERMUDA, SCORED IN THE FIRST NINE HOLES OF ONE ROUND *A TRIPLE BOGEY, A DOUBLE BOGEY, A BOGEY, A PAR, A BIRDIE, AN EAGLE, AND A HOLE IN ONE!* Oct. 11, 1975

**TORPEDOES** DROPPED INTO THE POTOMAC RIVER BY THE CONFEDERATES EARLY IN THE CIVIL WAR, CONSISTED OF A METAL CYLINDER FILLED WITH EXPLOSIVES, SUSPENDED BY ROPES FROM A *FLOATING BEER KEG*

THE **SECRETARY BIRD** CAN SWALLOW A HEN'S EGG WHOLE -- *WITHOUT BREAKING THE SHELL*

## 2,037 CIGARETTE LIGHTERS
COLLECTED AS GIFTS TO
BILL REPPERT, SR., OF ALLENTOWN, PA.,
*WHO DOESN'T SMOKE*
Submitted by Albert W. Caron,
Woodbridge, Virginia

**THE PRISON** in Athens, Greece,
IN WHICH SOCRATES WAS INCARCERATED,
IS STILL STANDING MORE THAN
*2,375 YEARS LATER*

### GHANDI
A PORTRAIT
MADE BY AN
INDIAN STUDENT
*WITH A
TYPEWRITER*

### LAMPREY EELS
CONSTRUCT NESTS 3 FT. HIGH
AND 4 FT. IN DIAMETER ON
THE SEA BOTTOM--*BOTH
PARENTS LABORING TOGETHER
TO CARRY HEAVY STONES*

**LEOPARDS** DEPRIVED OF THEIR PREY, WILL *EAT GRASS*

**12,000 GERMAN MERCENARIES** NEVER RETURNED TO THEIR HOMELAND AFTER FIGHTING FOR ENGLAND IN THE AMERICAN REVOLUTION. KING GEORGE III HAD AGREED TO PAY THE GERMAN DUKE OF BRUNSWICK **£7** FOR EACH SOLDIER KILLED.. AND A SIMILAR AMOUNT FOR EVERY 3 WOUNDED

**HIGH-RISE BIRDHOUSE** A BIRDHOUSE ERECTED BY GLEN TIMONEY, OF OAKLAND, ME., HAS 12 "APARTMENTS" AND IS MOUNTED ON A 35-FT. HIGH POLE WHICH HAS 17 MORE "APARTMENTS"

Submitted by Jules H. Marr, Albuquerque, N.M.

CHEEP RENT BIRD'S EYE VIEW HIGH RISE APARTMENTS "BIRDS ONLY"

THE **BRIDGE** ACROSS THE APURIMAC RIVER IN PERU, BUILT BY THE INCAS ABOUT 1350 AND SPANNING A 150-FT. GAP, WAS IN USE FOR MORE *THAN 500 YEARS*

**PRESIDENT WILLIAM HOWARD TAFT** IN 1910, IN A BASEBALL GAME BETWEEN THE WASHINGTON SENATORS AND PHILADELPHIA ATHLETICS, **STARTED THE PRESIDENTIAL CUSTOM OF THROWING OUT THE FIRST BALL**

THE **WINSTON CHURCHILL MEMORIAL AND LIBRARY** In Fulton, Mo., WAS BUILT FROM THE STONES OF THE CHURCH OF ST. MARY IN ALDERMANBURY, LONDON,-- *WHICH WAS RAZED BY FIRE IN 1666, AND AGAIN BY BOMBS IN WORLD WAR II*

**BUFFALO** IN CEYLON, OFTEN HAVE HORNS THAT CROSS, AND NATIVES BELIEVE THE LUCK OF THEIR OWNER WILL TAKE A TURN FOR THE BETTER WHEN HIS ANIMAL'S *HORNS CROSS*

GEN. PHILIP HENRY SHERIDAN (1831-1888) WHO BECAME COMMANDER OF THE U.S. ARMY AT 52, WAS ONLY A LIEU-TENANT BEFORE THE START OF THE CIVIL WAR

THE **CHURCH BELFRY** THAT NEVER HAD A CHURCH

*INNSWEILER*, A TOWN IN GERMANY, ERECTED A BELFRY IN 1877 BUT *HAS NEVER COLLECTED ENOUGH MONEY TO BUILD A CHURCH*

**AIME FELIX TSCHIFFELY** A SWISS SCHOOLMASTER, RODE HORSEBACK FROM BUENOS AIRES, ARGENTINA, TO WASHINGTON, D.C. -- *A DISTANCE OF 10,000 MILES* (1925-1927)

A TAVERN IN NEU-ISENBURG, GERMANY, IS SHAPED LIKE A HUGE PITCHER

THE **HOATZIN** A BIRD FOUND IN NORTHERN SO. AMERICA, HAS A HEAD LIKE THAT OF A SMALL *DONKEY*

**L**ADIES IN 16th AND 17th CENTURY ENGLAND, WORE THEIR WEDDING RING ON *THEIR THUMB*

**BYBLOS HARBOR** NEAR BEIRUT, LEBANON, HAS BEEN IN CONTINUOUS USE FOR 5,000 YEARS

132

**REAR ADMIRAL SIR GEORGE COCKBURN** OF THE BRITISH NAVY, WHO BURNED WASHINGTON, D.C. IN THE WAR OF 1812, ATTEMPTED TO HIRE AN AMERICAN HIGHWAYMAN, JOSEPH HARE, *TO KIDNAP PRESIDENT JAMES MADISON*

**THE CAVE CHURCH** IN OBERSTEIN, GERMANY, WAS DUG OUT OF A ROCKY MOUNTAIN AS AN ACT OF PENANCE BY A MAN WHO IN A QUARREL OVER A GIRL *KILLED HIS OWN BROTHER*

**DR. JOHN E. SMITH** STILL TEACHING MATHEMATICS AND PHYSICS AT EASTERN NEW MEXICO UNIV., IN PORTALES, N.M., *AT THE AGE OF 92* Submitted by Jules H. Marr, Albuquerque, N.M.

## GEORGE SAND (1804-1876)
THE CELEBRATED NOVELIST WHOSE REAL NAME WAS AMANDINE AURORE LUCIE DUDEVANT, NEVER WROTE IN THE DAYTIME -- *DOING ALL HER WORK BETWEEN THE HOURS OF 10 PM AND 5 AM*

## THE BELFRY
OF CHICHESTER CATHEDRAL, BUILT IN THE 15TH CENTURY, IS THE ONLY BELFRY OF AN ENGLISH CATHEDRAL *THAT IS NOT ATTACHED TO THE MAIN STRUCTURE*

## A $50 GOLD PIECE
OCTAGONAL IN SHAPE, LEGAL TENDER DURING THE CALIFORNIA GOLD RUSH, WAS POPULARLY CALLED A "SLUG"

## BAOBOB TREES
FOUND IN THE TROPICS, HAVE *TRUNKS 30 FEET IN DIAMETER*

## EIGHTY EIGHT
A TOWN IN KENTUCKY, IN THE 1948 PRESIDENTIAL ELECTION CAST 88 VOTES FOR DEWEY AND 88 VOTES FOR TRUMAN

**OXBURGH HALL** IN NORFOLK, ENGLAND, HAS BEEN OWNED BY THE SAME FAMILY FOR 490 YEARS

OH, NO!

**RAYMOND A. HUBLER** of New Albany, Ind., PITCHING FOR THE UNIVERSITY OF LOUISVILLE FRESHMAN BASEBALL TEAM, **STRUCK OUT 5 MEN IN ONE INNING** -- May, 1934

**THE TUATARA** FOUND ON ROCKY ISLETS OFF THE COAST OF NEW ZEALAND, IS THE ONLY SURVIVING MEMBER OF A FAMILY THAT INCLUDED THE DINOSAUR, ICHTHYOSAUR AND STEGOSAURUS 180,000,000 YEARS AGO

**HARRIET TUBMAN** A SPY FOR THE UNION ARMY IN THE CIVIL WAR FOR WHOSE CAPTURE THE SOUTH OFFERED $40,000 IN GOLD, *RECEIVED ONLY $200 IN PAY DURING 3 YEARS OF MILITARY SERVICE*

**THE PONTE ROTTO** IN ROME, ITALY, THE FIRST BRIDGE OVER THE TIBER RIVER, WAS IN *USE FOR 1,717 YEARS*

THE **MALE MIDWIFE TOAD** CARRIES THE EGGS LAID BY ITS MATE LIKE A BUNCH OF GRAPES ATTACHED TO ITS BACK

A **LIFE MASK** BEING MADE ON THOMAS JEFFERSON IN 1825, A YEAR BEFORE HIS DEATH, DRIED TOO QUICKLY AND HAD TO BE REMOVED WITH A *CHISEL AND MALLET*

**CHRISTOPHER GUSTAVUS MEMMINGER** SEC. OF THE TREASURY FOR THE CONFEDERATES, FOUND FUNDS SO LOW UPON HIS APPOINTMENT THAT *HE HAD TO BORROW A DESK*

**THE LILY PRINCE** A PAINTING ON THE WALLS OF THE PALACE OF Knossos, Crete, IS THE OLDEST KNOWN PICTURE OF A EUROPEAN --PAINTED 5,000 YEARS AGO

**GEORGE HALAS** COACHED IN THE NATIONAL FOOTBALL LEAGUE FOR 40 SEASONS-- LED THE CHICAGO BEARS TO 7 NFL CHAMPIONSHIPS-- ROLLED UP A TOTAL OF 320 VICTORIES-- AND SERVED AS OWNER, GENERAL MANAGER, RULES MAKER, TICKET MANAGER, PROMOTER, OFFICE MANAGER AND PLAYER

**THE WHEEL- BARROW ODOMETER** WAS USED IN NEW JERSEY IN 1907 TO MEASURE DISTANCES IN SURVEYS

**THE OLDEST BUILDING IN AUSTRALIA**
THE ELIZABETH FARM IN PARRAMATTA, AUSTRALIA, WAS BUILT IN 1794

**MALE CHAUVINISM IN THE YEAR 1225 B.C.**

A STATUE OF RAMESSES II AT KARNAK, EGYPT, IS COLOSSAL IN SIZE, WHILE THE FIGURE OF HIS WIFE IS *ONLY KNEE-HIGH*

A **LARGE MECHANICAL CAT** IS LOCATED IN THE WINDOW OF MANY RESTAURANTS IN TOKYO, JAPAN--*A MOVING ARM BECKONING PASSERSBY TO ENTER*

THE **SWASTIKA** LONG BEFORE IT WAS ADOPTED BY HITLER, *WAS USED AS AN EMBLEM BY 2 AMERICAN RAILROADS* -- THE ST. LOUIS, ROCKY MOUNTAIN AND PACIFIC R.R.; AND THE CHICAGO, ATTICA AND SOUTHERN R.R.

A **MOA EGG** FOUND IN FRAGMENTS IN THE SKELETON OF THE GIANT EXTINCT BIRD OF NEW ZEALAND, MEASURED, WHEN RESTORED, *7 INCHES IN LENGTH AND 5 INCHES IN DIAMETER*

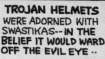

**TROJAN HELMETS** WERE ADORNED WITH SWASTIKAS -- IN THE BELIEF IT WOULD WARD OFF THE EVIL EYE ..

THE **VICUÑA** WAS HUNTED ONLY ONCE IN 4 YEARS BY THE ANCIENT INCAS -- AND ITS FLEECE COULD BE *USED ONLY BY ROYALTY*

**"Bourbon"** A ST. BERNARD DOG OWNED BY BRUCE CLEVENGER, OF KANSAS CITY, MO., *DAILY CARRIES THE CASH RECEIPTS FROM CLEVENGER'S SERVICE STATION TO THE UNITED MISSOURI BANK OF BLUE VALLEY*

**GLORIOSA** THE BIG BELL ON THE CATHEDRAL OF FRANKFORT ON THE MAIN, Germany, WEIGHING 26,290 POUNDS, *WAS CAST FROM THE METAL FROM FRENCH CANNON CAPTURED IN THE FRANCO-PRUSSIAN WAR*

A **CAMERA** MARKETED IN FRANCE, IN 1882, *WAS SHAPED LIKE A PISTOL*

**LIZZIE MURPHY** of Warren, R.I., PLAYED FIRST BASE ON MEN'S BASEBALL TEAMS THAT BARNSTORMED THE COUNTRY IN THE 1920's AND EARLY 1930's -- *FOR $5 A GAME*

THE **TWIN ELEPHANTS** PHILLIP ISLAND, AUSTRALIA, NATURAL ROCK FORMATION

**MRS. MARIE M. LIDDLE** OF ELMIRA, N.Y., WHO WAS BORN ON **APRIL 28, 1940,** IS THE MOTHER OF 2 CHILDREN, JULIE LIDDLE, BORN **APRIL 28, 1967** AND WILLIAM LIDDLE, BORN **APRIL 28, 1969**

## JEAN-PAUL SARTRE
THE FRENCH NOVELIST, PLAYWRIGHT AND "FATHER OF EXISTENTIALISM" *TAUGHT HIMSELF TO READ AND WRITE*

THE **SIAMESE TREES** St. Augustine, Florida, AN OAK TREE *WITH A PALM TREE GROWING FROM IT*

## EACH VIOLIN
MADE BY BRYANT WEST, OF PHILLIP ISLAND, AUSTRALIA, CONTAINS **70** DIFFERENT PIECES OF WOOD, *INCLUDING ENGLISH WILLOW, SWISS PINE, EBONY FROM CEYLON, EUROPEAN ROSEWOOD AND MAPLE, AND SILVER SPRUCE FROM ALASKA*

## YOUNG DONKEYS
OWNED BY THE DULANIS OF THE YARKAND REGION OF CHINA, HAVE GARTERS TIED TO EACH LEG-- *TO PROTECT THEM FROM EVIL SPIRITS*

**ENNA CASTLE** In Southern Tyrol, Italy, HAS BEEN OCCUPIED BY THE SAME FAMILY FOR 328 YEARS

**GEORGE WESTINGHOUSE** (1846-1914) THE INVENTOR, ENGINEER AND MANUFACTURER, IN 1871, INTRODUCED SATURDAY AFTERNOONS OFF FOR HIS WORKMEN-- AND VACATIONS WITH PAY

*MONEY THAT WENT UP IN SMOKE!* **TOBACCO** IN COLONIAL VIRGINIA, WAS THE PRINCIPAL MEDIUM OF EXCHANGE

**NATURE'S CEMETERY** WESTERN AUSTRALIA, NEAR PERTH, NATURAL STONE PINNACLES, *SHAPED LIKE TOMBSTONES*

THE **MALE SOCIETY FINCH** HAS EXACTLY THE SAME MARKINGS AS THE FEMALE --*WHICH IT CONSTANTLY SERENADES*

**4 ANCIENT CASTLES** in Lastours, France, SHARE THE SAME ROCKY SLOPE OF THE BLACK MOUNTAINS

**CAPTAIN PETER PARKER** OF THE BRITISH NAVY, WHO WAS SLAIN BY YANKEE MILITIAMEN ON KENT ISLAND, NEAR BALTIMORE, MARYLAND IN THE WAR OF 1812, WAS THE ONLY HIGH-RANKING ENEMY NAVAL OFFICER KILLED ON AMERICAN SOIL

HIS BODY WAS SHIPPED HOME-- PRESERVED IN A CASK OF JAMAICA RUM

**SAM MITCHEL** of Roslyn, N.Y., A MEMBER OF ENGINEERS C.C., MADE 6 HOLES IN ONE IN THE PERIOD OF ONE YEAR

THE **BLACKFISH** (Tautoga onitis) A MOTTLED SALTWATER GAME FISH, HAS 2 SETS OF TEETH, WITH WHICH IT CRUSHES SHELLFISH

**MT AIGUILLE** in the Swiss Alps, SO STEEP IT HAS GIVEN ITS NAME TO ANY ROCKY PEAK SHAPED LIKE A NEEDLE, WAS FIRST CLIMBED IN 1492. *IT WAS NOT CONQUERED AGAIN FOR 342 YEARS*

**WYSTAN HUGH AUDEN** (1907-1973,) THE BRITISH-AMERICAN POET, MARRIED ERIKA MANN, DAUGHTER OF NOVELIST THOMAS MANN, TO ENABLE HER TO LEAVE NAZI GERMANY. THEY HAD NEVER MET PREVIOUS TO THEIR MARRIAGE, YET THEY REMAINED WEDDED UNTIL HER DEATH *33 YEARS LATER*

SCHOOL IS OUT
TEACHER HAS
GONE HOME

*Epitaph* OF S.B. McCRACKEN, A TEACHER, IN ELKHART, IND.

**CHARLES L. WAGNER** of Shelbyville, Ill., WHO BECAME ONE OF AMERICA'S LEADING CONCERT MANAGERS, USED AS HIS DESK A **CONVERTED GRAND PIANO**

144

**THE STORK'S HELPER**
CHILDLESS WIVES AMONG THE PENNSYLVANIA DUTCH, ONCE PLACED A CHARM IN THE SHAPE OF A FROG IN THEIR BEDROOMS IN THE BELIEF IT *COULD ASSURE CHILDREN*

AN **INKWELL** USED BY PRESIDENT THEODORE ROOSEVELT, WAS THE HOLLOWED OUT FOOT OF A *RHINOCEROS*

**CONTINENTAL CURRENCY**
WHICH GAVE RISE TO THE PHRASE "NOT WORTH A CONTINENTAL," FROM 1775 UNTIL 1781 PAID MORE THAN 75% OF THE COST OF THE AMERICAN REVOLUTION

**PRESIDENT JOHN TYLER**
THE 10TH CHIEF EXECUTIVE OF THE UNITED STATES, WAS SO BITTERLY DISLIKED BY CONGRESS THAT IT WOULD NOT ALLOCATE FUNDS TO *REPLACE PATCHED CARPETING AND TATTERED DRAPES IN THE WHITE HOUSE*

**WILLOW BASKETS**
ARE USED BY FISHERMEN OF CHIOGGIA, ITALY, TO KEEP FISH FRESH BY LOWERING THEM INTO THE SEA

**THE DUKE OF ALVA** (1508-1582), HAVING SUPPRESSED A REVOLT IN THE NETHERLANDS FOR KING PHILIP II, of Spain, BOASTED UPON HIS RETURN THAT HE HAD EXECUTED *18,000 VICTIMS*

**CHIEF SITTING BULL** THE INDIAN CREDITED WITH WIPING OUT CUSTER'S FORCES, *ACTUALLY WAS A MEDICINE MAN AND STAYED BEHIND THE LINES AT LITTLE BIG HORN*

A "WILD SPINACH" TREE" *12 FEET TALL* ... Grown by Barney Roybal, Bell, California

A NEW VOLCANO ON TRISTAN DA CUNHA ISLAND IN THE ATLANTIC--*IT ROSE TO A HEIGHT OF 90 FEET IN A FEW HOURS* (Oct. 10, 1961)

JAPANESE CHERRY BLOSSOMS COME IN 50 DIFFERENT VARIETIES

GENERAL ULYSSES S. GRANT COMMANDER-IN-CHIEF OF THE UNION ARMY IN THE CIVIL WAR, AND 18th PRESIDENT OF THE UNITED STATES, *DISLIKED MILITARY PARADES AND MARTIAL MUSIC, AND REFUSED TO LISTEN TO OFF-COLOR STORIES*

MACISTE A STAR IN ITALIAN MOVIES FOR 10 YEARS, HAD BEEN AN ILLITERATE FURNITURE MOVER WHO COULD *BARELY WRITE HIS OWN NAME*

**FEODOR DOSTOEVSKY** (1821-1881) THE FAMED RUSSIAN NOVELIST, SENTENCED TO DEATH FOR POLITICAL CONSPIRACY, WAS REPRIEVED BY A COURIER FROM THE CZAR *WHEN HE WAS ON THE SCAFFOLD*

**SAMUEL ADAMS** WHO ORGANIZED THE BOSTON TEA PARTY TO PROTEST BRITISH TAXES ON THE COLONISTS, WAS IN 1764 *THE BOSTON TAX COLLECTOR*

**THE TARSIER** A SMALL PRIMATE FOUND IN THE PHILIPPINES AND BORNEO, *CAN LEAP 7 FEET*

**MIRACLE ROCK** IN Glade Park, Colo., A HUGE VASE-SHAPED ROCK NEARLY 70 FEET HIGH AND WEIGHING 12,000 TONS, *BALANCES ON THE EDGE OF A PRECIPICE ON A TINY BASE*

**EMILY DICKINSON** (1830-1886) THE POET -- CONSIDERED HERSELF SO UGLY, THAT WHEN CONVERSING WITH A VISITOR IN HER HOME, *SHE ALWAYS REMAINED IN ANOTHER ROOM, TALKING THROUGH AN OPEN DOOR*

**ROBERT DOTZAUER** OF CEDAR RAPIDS, IOWA, A SWIMMER FOR ONLY 2 YEARS, SWAM THE LENGTH OF A POOL 25 YARDS-- ON HIS BACK, *BALANCING A LADDER ON HIS CHIN*

Submitted by Dan Miller, Cedar Rapids

A **PUMPKIN** GROWN BY Edgar Van Wyck of Roland, Manitoba, *WEIGHED 353 LBS.*

THE **GRAVE MARKER** OF A CHIPPEWA INDIAN BORE NO IDENTIFYING NAME -- ONLY HIS CLAN TOTEM, A MARTEN, *HEAD DOWNWARD AS A SIGN OF DEATH*

**PETER COOPER·**
(1791-1883)
WHO FOUNDED,
COOPER UNION,
THE ADULT
EDUCATION INSTITUTE
IN NEW YORK CITY,
HAD HIMSELF RECEIVED
NO FORMAL EDUCATION,
AND REMAINED
*VIRTUALLY ILLITERATE
ALL HIS LIFE*

**THE FIRST PRACTICAL STEAM ENGINE** INVENTED BY THOMAS SAVERY IN 1698, WAS USED *TO PUMP WATER FROM FLOODED MINE SHAFTS*

**ADMIRAL THOMAS FRANCIS FREMANTLE**
(1765-1819) of the British Navy,
*WAS THE FATHER*
OF AN ADMIRAL--
*THE GRANDFATHER*
OF AN ADMIRAL AND
*THE GREAT-GRANDFATHER*
OF AN ADMIRAL--
THE FOUR GENERATIONS
SERVED CONTINUOUSLY
FOR 151 YEARS

**CARRIAGES** IN THE U.S. IN THE EARLY 19th CENTURY WERE SUBJECT TO A FEDERAL TAX --THE DUTY VARYING WITH THE VEHICLE'S SIZE--A ONE-HORSE SHAY PAID $3 A YEAR

**CHARLES FROHMAN** (1860-1915), THE BROADWAY PRODUCER, WHO MANAGED 28 STARS, OWNED ONE THEATER AND CONTROLLED 5 OTHERS, AT DEATH LEFT A NET ESTATE OF **$451**

THE **GLENESSLIN**, A BRITISH MERCHANT SCHOONER, WAS DELIBERATELY WRECKED ON OCT. 1, 1913 AT NEAHKANIE, OREGON, BY HER CAPTAIN, WHO ORDERED FULL SAIL, SET A COURSE TOWARD LAND AND THREATENED ANYONE WHO CHANGED COURSE WITH A CHARGE OF MUTINY

**ANTONIO GILLETTE** AN ACROBAT, DID A BACKFLIP IN 1903 ON THE OVER-HANGING ROCK AT GLACIER POINT, CALIF., *3,214 FT. ABOVE YOSEMITE VALLEY*

**A PORTABLE OBSERVATION TOWER** 30 FEET HIGH, THAT WORKED LIKE A PAIR OF TONGS, WAS PROPOSED BY A MILITARY WRITER NAMED STOCQUELER IN 1854, FOR USE BY THE BRITISH IN THE SIEGE OF SEBASTOPOL

**RICHARD PRICE** (1723-1791), THE ENGLISH POLITICAL PHILOSOPHER, LAID THE FOUNDATION FOR ACTUARIAL TABLES USED IN MODERN LIFE INSURANCE AND PENSIONS *204 YEARS AGO*

THE "NIAGARA" OLIVER HAZARD PERRY'S BATTLESHIP THAT WON CONTROL OF LAKE ERIE IN THE WAR OF 1812, WAS SCUTTLED AT THE END OF THAT WAR —BUT RAISED FOR OBSERVANCE OF THE BATTLE'S 100th ANNIVERSARY

EGYPTIAN PRINCESSES IN ANCIENT TIMES, WORE CORSETS CREATED BY *WRAPPING BINDING CLOTH TIGHTLY AROUND THEIR WAISTS*

USED SETS OF FALSE TEETH WERE ADVERTISED FOR IN THE 1800's IN LONDON, ENGLAND

OLD ARTIFICIAL TEETH BOUGHT.—
MESSRS BROWNING.

THE GREAT BLUE HERON CATCHES FISH BY *SPEARING THEM WITH ITS BILL*

THE GRAVES of the Hajerai, of Chad, Africa, ARE ALWAYS ON A HILLTOP, AND ALWAYS ADORNED WITH A CLAY PITCHER AND A CONICAL STONE

**A POPULAR COIFFURE** in France, AFTER ITS NAVAL VICTORIES OF 1778, FEATURED *A HUGE SHIP*

**COAL MINERS** OF FRANCE AND ENGLAND, IN THE 18TH CENTURY, OFTEN *WERE WOMEN AND CHILDREN*

**17-YEAR LOCUSTS** ACTUALLY REQUIRE 17 YEARS TO DEVELOP--YET, *AS ADULTS, LIVE ONLY 30 TO 40 DAYS*

FRED J. SIMON
OF LINCOLN, ILL.,
MADE A SLIDE FOR A
BOLO TIE FROM TWO
30-CALIBER BULLETS
--ONE OF WHICH PIERCED
THE OTHER IN THE AIR

THE **OLDEST WRAPPER** FROM A PACKAGE OF TOBACCO -PRINTED IN VIRGINIA, IN 1644

Orien-tal!    Virginia Tobak
'tNicholas Desbrecht sold tobacco Amsterdam 1644

JEAN DU SABLE
(1745-1818)
WHO FOUNDED
CHICAGO,
BUILDING THE
FIRST HOUSE
ON ITS SITE IN
1779, *WAS A
BLACK WHO
BECAME WEALTHY
TRADING WITH
THE INDIANS*

**LORNE GASCHO**
OF ELKTON, MICH.,
RECEIVED A POSTCARD
FEB. 3, 1976 THAT HAD BEEN
MAILED TO HIS GRANDFATHER
FROM CHICAGO, ILL.,
*ON JAN. 7, 1908* --
THE POSTCARD, ENROUTE
FOR 68 YEARS, WAS DELIVERED
WITHOUT A "POSTAGE DUE"
ALTHOUGH IT CARRIED ONLY
A ONE-CENT STAMP

**THE OAK TREE OF THE VIRGIN**
NEAR VIROFLAY, FRANCE,
HAS HAD A STATUE OF THE
VIRGIN IN ITS TRUNK FOR
*MORE THAN 100 YEARS*

**A FICKLE FEMALE**
A GIRL BEING TATTOOED,
CHANGED HER MIND
ABOUT WHICH BOYFRIEND
SHE PREFERRED, AND
ENDED UP WITH 3
NAMES ON HER ARM--
*TWO WITH A LINE
DRAWN THROUGH THEM*

**THE ANCIENT
MURRELET**
Found in the
Aleutian Islands,
IS CALLED
"ANCIENT" BECAUSE
ITS HEAD ALWAYS HAS
**STREAKS OF WHITE**

**LUELLA GEER**
OF RAVENNA, OHIO,
WAS FITTED WITH FALSE
TEETH IN 1895, AND WAS
STILL WEARING THE SAME
DENTAL PLATE WITHOUT
ADJUSTMENT OR REPAIR
*80 YEARS LATER*
SUBMITTED BY RICHARD C.
HOUSE, LA CANADA, CALIF.

**ED**
*SCHIEFFELIN*
A
PROSPECTOR
IN SOUTHERN
ARIZONA
IN THE 1870's,
WARNED
THAT HE
WAS MORE
APT TO
FIND A
TOMBSTONE
THAN
RICHES,
*NAMED
THE MINE
HE FOUND
TOMBSTONE,*

IT YIELDED
$40,000,000
IN SILVER
AND
$3,000,000
IN GOLD

A **PORTABLE DRESSING
TENT**
ADVERTISED
IN LONDON, ENGLAND,
IN THE 1920's,
WAS SUPPORTED
BY A TOP SHAPED LIKE
A LAMP-SHADE
*THAT RESTED
ON THE
BATHER'S HEAD*

**QUEEN ELIZABETH I**
OF ENGLAND, HAD 2,000 GOWNS --
WHICH WERE KEPT IN A SEPARATE
*CLOTHING HOUSE*

"LAUGHING JACK" A STATUE ABOVE
A WELL IN A VINEYARD IN GERMANY'S
TAUNUS MTS., CARRIES THE INSCRIPTION:
"May your drink be blessed, water
for you and wine for me."

**ARTHUR E. GEHRKE**
OF WATERTOWN, WIS.,
FOR A PERIOD OF 23 YEARS
HIBERNATED EACH WINTER
--STAYING IN BED FROM
*THANKSGIVING DAY
UNTIL EASTER*

**SIR WILLIAM BLACKSTONE**
(1723-1780)
AUTHOR OF THE MOST INFLUENTIAL BOOK IN ENGLISH LAW, *NEVER PRACTICED LAW HIMSELF*

**TOKEN PENNIES** ISSUED BY NORTHERN MERCHANTS DURING THE CIVIL WAR WERE USED AS PENNIES, BUT WERE INSCRIBED "NOT ONE CENT"

**MARSHALL F. FISH**
REELECTED TOWN CLERK OF WESTPORT, N.Y., IN 1973, FOUND THAT HE AND HIS OPPONENT, RICHARD PAQUETTE, IN DISTRICT 2, RECEIVED THESE TOTALS ON ITS 2 VOTING MACHINES:

|  | FISH | PAQUETTE |
|---|---|---|
| MACHINE #1 | 145 | 145 |
| MACHINE #2 | 142 | 142 |

**JAMES E. WARD**
of La Grange, N.C., ENLISTED IN THE U.S. ARMY AT 14, SERVED 2 YEARS, INCLUDING 5 MONTHS IN COMBAT IN KOREA, WAS MADE A SERGEANT -- *THEN WAS DISCHARGED AS UNDERAGE*

**SALAD BOWLS** USED BY NATIVES OF BORNEO ARE SHAPED LIKE A DOG *IN THE BELIEF IT WILL PREVENT STOMACHACHES*

**GEORGES BIZET** (1838-1875) FAMED FOR HIS OPERA, "CARMEN," WAS SO WEAKENED BY REHEARSALS FOR ITS PREMIERE, *THAT HE DIED JUST 3 MONTHS LATER AT THE AGE OF 36*

A **BRIDE** IN THE BASOKO TRIBE IN THE CONGO, IS CARRIED BY FRIENDS ON A LITTER TO HER WEDDING, SUPPORTED THROUGHOUT THE CEREMONY AND THEN CARRIED TO HER NEW HOME

**THE RUINED CASTLE** NEAR SAAZ, CZECHOSLOVAKIA, *NATURAL ROCK FORMATION*

THE **CARPENTER FROG** HAS A CROAK THAT SOUNDS LIKE THE *BLOW OF A HAMMER*

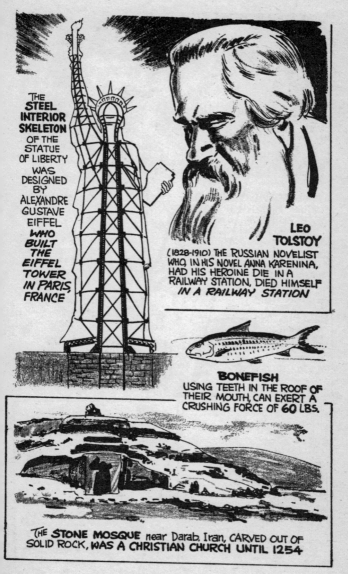

THE **STEEL INTERIOR SKELETON** OF THE **STATUE OF LIBERTY** WAS DESIGNED BY **ALEXANDRE GUSTAVE EIFFEL** *WHO BUILT THE EIFFEL TOWER IN PARIS, FRANCE*

**LEO TOLSTOY** (1828-1910) THE RUSSIAN NOVELIST WHO, IN HIS NOVEL ANNA KARENINA, HAD HIS HEROINE DIE IN A RAILWAY STATION, DIED HIMSELF *IN A RAILWAY STATION*

**BONEFISH** USING TEETH IN THE ROOF OF THEIR MOUTH, CAN EXERT A CRUSHING FORCE OF 60 LBS.

THE **STONE MOSQUE** near Darab, Iran, CARVED OUT OF SOLID ROCK, WAS A CHRISTIAN CHURCH UNTIL 1254

**THE ORIGINAL CLUBHOUSE** OF THE PRESTIGIOUS NEW YORK YACHT CLUB BUILT IN HOBOKEN, NEW JERSEY, IN 1846, WAS A *SMALL WOODEN BUILDING*

**TODWADDLE** A TOWN IN N.Y. STATE, WAS NAMED FOR TOD NELSON, WHO WAS SO FAT, FOLKS LIKED TO *WATCH TOD WADDLE*

**EHMANN LAJOS** OF MOHÁCS, HUNGARY, BY MICRO-WRITING, *WROTE 32 LINES OF WORDS ON A SINGLE MATCH STICK*

**THE PIED-BILL GREBE** (*Podilymbus podiceps*) BUILDS HER NEST IN THE FORM OF A RAFT--*ATTACHED TO REEDS SO IT WILL NOT FLOAT AWAY*

**A STAND OF WHEAT** IN *WAITSBURG, WASH.,* IN 1908, WAS CUT IN THE FIELD, HAULED TO A MILL, GROUND INTO FLOUR, AND BAKED INTO BISCUITS--*ALL IN 22 MINUTES* Submitted by Jerry Maioli, Walla Walla, Wash.

THE **WADDELL VILLA** WHICH STOOD ON THE CORNER OF 5th AVE. AND 37th ST., IN N.Y.C., WAS FAMOUS IN THE 1800's FOR ITS GRAND PARTIES, BUT MRS. WILLIAM H.C. WADDELL LOST HER FORTUNE IN THE PANIC OF 1857, AND SPENT HER OLD AGE IN ONE ROOM IN A HOTEL

**LOUIS BRAILLE** THE FRENCHMAN WHO INVENTED A SYSTEM OF READING FOR THE BLIND, ADAPTED IT FROM MESSAGES USED BY FRENCH TROOPS WHO PUNCHED MARKS IN THICK PAPER SO THEY *COULD BE READ AT NIGHT BY FEEL WITH- OUT USE OF A LIGHT*

THE **MOUNTAIN CHURCH** OF ROJEN, IN THE ITALIAN TYROL, WAS BUILT BY A FARMER ON THE EDGE OF A PRECIPICE OVER WHICH A WAGON BEARING HIS TWO CHILDREN PLUNGED -- *YET BOTH SURVIVED*

THE **LOP-EARED SHEEP** of North Africa, HAS A COAT THAT IS *HALF WOOL AND HALF HAIR*

THE **DOME** of the CAPITOL OF KENTUCKY, AT FRANKFORT, IS A REPLICA OF NAPOLEON'S TOMB IN PARIS, FRANCE

## FANNY THORNE

OF PRESTON CANDOVER, ENGLAND, SHOCKED AN 8-ACRE FIELD OF BARLEY SINGLE-HANDEDLY IN 11½ HOURS IN 1949 *AT THE AGE OF 86*

**MARSHALL F. FISH**
OF WESTPORT, N.Y., HOLDING A RIFLE UPSIDE DOWN, WITH THE BUTT RESTING ON HIS HEAD, CAN *SPLIT THE EDGE OF ONIONSKIN PAPER AT A DISTANCE OF 27 FEET*

Submitted by Mayor Donald L. McIntyre of Westport

164

**FLORENCE LAWRENCE** IN 1908, BECAME THE FIRST **MOVIE STAR** TO BECOME **KNOWN TO THE PUBLIC!** PREVIOUSLY THE TRUE IDENTITIES OF ALL FILM PLAYERS WERE KEPT SECRET SO THE PRODUCERS COULD KEEP THEIR SALARIES LOW

**SHOES** IN COLONIAL AMERICA COULD BE WORN **ON EITHER FOOT**

**NASSAU HALL** AT PRINCETON UNIVERSITY, IN NEW JERSEY, IN 1789 *WAS THE LARGEST BUILDING IN THE COUNTRY*

THE **"MOTH WITH A "HORN"** A BRITISH MOTH EMITS A SQUEAKY WARNING IN FLIGHT BY ALTERNATELY DRAWING IN AND EXPELLING AIR THROUGH ITS PROBOSCIS

**"TOTO"** A DOG OWNED BY ROLAND FRANK, OF HAMILTON, MICH., GAVE BIRTH TO ONE PUPPY ON APRIL 3, 1970 -THEN HAD **4 MORE PUPS 30 DAYS LATER**

**THE FLYING GURNARD**
HAS ENORMOUS WINGLIKE
PECTORAL FINS, BUT
*IT CANNOT FLY*

Mr. & Mrs. **JOSEPH MEYERBERG**
of Brooklyn, N.Y.,
DISCOVERED
AFTER THEIR MARRIAGE
THAT HER SOCIAL
SECURITY NUMBER WAS
**064-01-8089**
AND HIS WAS
**064-01-8090**

**DANIEL O'LEARY**
OF Chicago, Ill.,
AT THE AGE
OF **63**
WALKED A
MILE AN
HOUR FOR
**1,000
CONSECUTIVE
HOURS.**
Cincinnati,
Ohio, 1907

The **OLD WOMAN OF FRANCONIA**
Franconia Notch, N.H.,
*NATURAL STONE FORMATION*

THE BASILICA of SANTA MARIA LA MENOR IN THE DOMINICAN REPUBLIC, WAS THE FIRST CATHEDRAL IN AMERICA *RAISED TO THAT STATUS IN 1546*

**CHARLES ROBERT LOCKHART** STATE TREASURER OF TEXAS IN THE 1930's, WAS A *3-FOOT, 9-INCH MIDGET*

TY COBB WHO IN 1913 WAS THE HIGHEST-SALARIED OUTFIELDER IN BASEBALL, *WAS PAID $12,000 A YEAR*

167

## CHARLES NESSLER
INVENTED THE PERMANENT WAVE, WHICH MADE MILLIONS OF DOLLARS FOR BEAUTY PARLORS, YET WHEN HE DIED IN 1951 **ONLY ONE HAIR-DRESSER ATTENDED HIS FUNERAL**

## THE HAUGHWOUT BUILDING
A 5-STORY DEPARTMENT STORE IN NEW YORK CITY HAD THE FIRST PASSENGER ELEVATOR IN THE U.S.        (1857)

THE **SKULL** OF GENERAL LOUIS JOSEPH DE MONTCALM, WHO WAS MORTALLY WOUNDED AT QUEBEC IN 1759, **IS EXHIBITED IN A GLASS CASE IN THE CHAPEL OF THE URSULINE NUNS**

**ELLEN ELIZABETH BENSON** OF NEW YORK, N.Y., AT THE AGE OF 12 HAD *AN I.Q. OF 214*

THE **BLACKSMITH FROG** (Hyla faber) HAS A CALL THAT SOUNDS LIKE A **SLEDGE HITTING AN ANVIL**

"WASHINGTON CROSSING THE DELAWARE" WAS PAINTED BY EMANUEL LEUTZE WHO WON FAME FOR HIS SCENES FROM AMERICAN HISTORY--*BUT HE SPENT MOST OF HIS ADULT LIFE IN GERMANY*

A STRIPED BARBER POLE 12 FEET HIGH, MADE FROM A CEDAR LOG, WITHSTOOD THE 1904 FIRE *THAT DESTROYED EVERY MAJOR DOWNTOWN BUILDING IN BALTIMORE, MD.*

**AMERICA'S SMALLEST PRESIDENT**
James Madison
THE 4th PRESIDENT OF THE UNITED STATES *WAS UNDER 5'6" TALL AND WEIGHED BUT 100 LBS.*

A **HUGE WHITE ELEPHANT**
BUILT NEAR ATLANTIC
CITY, N.J., IN 1882 AS A
*10-ROOM HOTEL*

**RAY HIBBELER**
of Chicago, Ill., FOR WRITING THE
SONG, "TELL ME YOU'LL FORGIVE ME,"
RECEIVED A ROYALTY CHECK IN
1926 *FOR ONE CENT*

**AINU**
**WOMEN**
OF JAPAN,
ALWAYS COVER
THEIR MOUTH WITH
ONE HAND WHEN
*SPEAKING TO*
*A MAN*

**FRIEDRICH WILHELM FROEBEL** (1782-1852) THE GERMAN EDUCATOR, FOUNDED THE FIRST KINDERGARTEN IN 1837-- BUT CONSIDERED HIMSELF A FAILURE BECAUSE THE *PRUSSIAN GOVERNMENT BANNED KINDERGARTENS AS "SOCIALISTIC"*

**TUMBLE DOLLS** WERE ORIGINATED BY THE CHINESE WHO MADE THEM IN THE IMAGE OF BUDDHA WITH WEIGHTED BOTTOMS TO ILLUSTRATE THEIR BELIEF THAT *BUDDHA COULD NOT FALL*

**MALE SILKWORM MOTHS** HAVE A SENSE OF SMELL SO KEEN THAT THEY CAN DETECT A FEMALE MOTH MORE THAN *6 MILES AWAY*

**THE STATE CAPITOL** in Madison, Wisc., *HAS THE LARGEST GRANITE DOME OF ANY BUILDING IN THE U.S.*

# JAMES A. GARFIELD
( 1831 - 1881 )
ON NOVEMBER 2, 1880 WAS *SIMULTANEOUSLY QUALIFIED FOR 3 HIGH FEDERAL POSTS*.. HE WAS A REPRESENTATIVE FROM OHIO, HAD BEEN ELECTED A U.S. SENATOR, AND WAS PRESIDENT-ELECT OF THE U.S.

**ST. LUKE'S CHURCH**
AT SMITHFIELD, VA.,
IS THE OLDEST UNRESTORED
CHURCH IN THE U.S. (1632)

AN **EGG BEATER** USED IN COLONIAL AMERICA, WHISKED THE EGG BY TURNING THE BEATER WITH THE STRING OF A BOW

**PHILIP JOHNSON**
OF WASTEDO, MINN., HAS LIVED IN THE SAME HOUSE FOR **100 YEARS**
Submitted by Marvin Broin, Goodhue, Minn.

172

**ELIZABETH BLACKWELL**
(1821-1910)
THE FIRST WOMAN DOCTOR OF MEDICINE IN MODERN TIMES, *OPPOSED VACCINATION*

*THE* **JINXED BUILDING!**
FORD'S THEATER IN WASH., D.C., IN WHICH PRES. LINCOLN WAS SHOT IN 1865, WAS CONVERTED INTO AN OFFICE BUILDING WHICH COLLAPSED 28 YEARS LATER, **BURYING HUNDREDS OF CLERKS BENEATH TONS OF DEBRIS**

THE **CORKSCREW TREE**

Submitted by Abigail Merriam, Greenfield, Mass.

*THE* **LARGEST LAND GRANT IN THE WORLD**
LUCIEN MAXWELL OWNED A SECTION OF NEW MEXICO THAT STRETCHED FROM SPRINGER TO THE LAS ANIMUS RIVER, FROM ELIZABETHTOWN TO RATON-- A TOTAL OF **1,714,764** ACRES

**THE DRAGONFLY** CAN SEE A FLYING GNAT AT A DISTANCE OF 18 FEET

**A BALLOON** PROPOSED FOR TRANSATLANTIC FLIGHTS BY PROFESSOR CARLINCOURT LOWE, OF NEW YORK CITY, WAS TO BE EQUIPPED WITH A LIFEBOAT POWERED BY A COAL ENGINE   (1860)

**TLALOC** THE PRE-AZTEC RAIN GOD EXCAVATED IN MEXICO IN 1963, WAS MOVED 30 MILES TO ITS PRESENT SITE IN MEXICO CITY-- AND ON THAT DAY *THE CITY SUFFERED ONE OF THE HEAVIEST RAIN-STORMS IN ITS HISTORY*

**ADJUSTABLE WOOD CANDLESTICK** USED IN COLONIAL AMERICA

**HORATIUS,** AN ELEPHANT, SHIPPED TO CANADA FROM TROPICAL INDIA, WAS OUT-FITTED FOR CANADIAN WINTERS *WITH EARMUFFS, A SPECIAL BLANKET AND OVERSHOES*

## A BALLOON

IN WHICH SWEDISH EXPLORER S.A. ANDRÉE AND 2 COMPANIONS TOOK OFF FROM SPITZBERGEN TO THE NORTH POLE IN 1897, WAS FOUND 33 YEARS LATER PERFECTLY PRESERVED BENEATH THE ARCTIC ICE --WITH EVEN PHOTOGRAPHS TAKEN BY THE EXPEDITION INTACT

HERE LIES
HENRY BEYLE
OF Milam...
I LIVED, I WROTE,
I LOVED

**Epitaph** OF STENDHAL (1783-1842) THE NOVELIST -- WHOSE NAME WAS ACTUALLY MARIE HENRI BEYLE, AND WAS FRENCH --ALTHOUGH HIS EPITAPH IS IN ITALIAN AND GIVES HIS BIRTHPLACE AS MILAN

## PERPETUAL POCKET CALENDARS

MADE OF SILVER, WERE AVAILABLE IN EUROPE IN THE 17th CENTURY

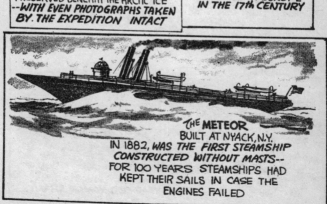

**THE METEOR**
BUILT AT NYACK, N.Y. IN 1882, WAS THE FIRST STEAMSHIP CONSTRUCTED WITHOUT MASTS-- FOR 100 YEARS STEAMSHIPS HAD KEPT THEIR SAILS IN CASE THE ENGINES FAILED

A **TOMB** NEAR DAMASCUS, SYRIA, IS VISITED ANNUALLY BY THOUSANDS OF PILGRIMS WHO BELIEVE IT IS THAT OF ABEL, *THE SON OF ADAM AND EVE*

THE **ARMY** OF MONTENEGRO, ONE OF THE REPUBLICS OF YUGOSLAVIA, FOR **500** YEARS HAS COMPRISED THE COUNTRY'S *ENTIRE MALE POPULATION*

**YOUNG GIRLS** IN AMERICA, IN THE 1850's, ACHIEVED TIGHT CURLS BY *ROLLING THEIR LOCKS OF HAIR AROUND WOODEN STICKS*

A **MODERN BRIDGE** ERECTED NEAR Canicade, Portugal, *ABOVE A 1700-YEAR-OLD ROMAN SPAN*

THE TOWN HALL OF MOSBACH, GERMANY, UNTIL THE MIDDLE OF THE 16TH CENTURY, WAS THE CHURCH OF ST. CECELIA

JOHN KANE of Pittsburgh, Pa, WHO BECAME A CELEBRATED ARTIST, *STARTED AS A HOUSE PAINTER*

AARON BURR (1756-1836). AFTER KILLING ALEXANDER HAMILTON IN A DUEL, COMPLETED HIS TERM AS *VICE-PRES.* OF THE U.S., ALTHOUGH *INDICTED FOR MURDER IN BOTH NEW YORK AND NEW JERSEY*

**M. CHEVREUL** A FRENCHMAN, IN 1886 WAS THE SUBJECT OF THE FIRST PHOTO INTERVIEW --CONDUCTED BY PAUL NADAR-- *ON THE EVE OF CHEVREUL'S 101st BIRTHDAY*

A **FLY** MOVES ITS WINGS AT THE RATE OF **330** STROKES A SECOND

THE **"WHITE SUGAR" SANDS OF ALAMOGORDO** THE ROLLING DUNES OF THE DESERT WEST OF ALAMOGORDO, NEW MEXICO, COVERING SOME 270 SQ. MILES, LOOK LIKE *MOUNDS OF GRANULATED SUGAR*

THE **U.S. NAVAL ACADEMY** at Annapolis, Md., OPENED IN 1845 IN FT. SEVERN--*AN OUTMODED POST DONATED TO IT BY THE ARMY*

**RUTH PONTICO**
A SIDESHOW ATTRACTION OF THE ROYAL AMUSEMENT SHOWS, WEIGHED 815 POUNDS, AND SHE WAS THE DAUGHTER OF A CIRCUS FAT LADY AND THE GRAND-DAUGHTER OF A CIRCUS FAT LADY

**SAIHOJI PARK**
IN A ZEN MONASTERY NEAR KYOTO, JAPAN, HAS BEEN A RESTFUL GLADE FOR 600 YEARS

**THE DOVE FOUNTAIN** in Feuchtwangen, Germany, MARKS THE SPOT WHERE CHARLEMAGNE LOST WHILE HUNTING, WAS GUIDED TO A SPRING BY A DOVE

**VINCENT YOUMANS**
THE SONGWRITER WHO COMPOSED "TEA FOR TWO," DREAMT THAT HIS MOTHER TOLD HIM HE WAS DYING OF T.B.-- A HALF HOUR LATER HE WAS STRICKEN WITH HIS FIRST HEMORRHAGE, AND EVENTUALLY DIED OF TUBERCULOSIS

A **RECEPTION HALL** PLANNED IN 1758 BY M. CHARLES RIBART AS A TRIBUTE TO KING LOUIS XV of France, WAS TO HAVE BEEN IN THE SHAPE OF AN ELEPHANT

THE **HORNED TOAD** LOOKS FEROCIOUS, BUT HAS A MILD DISPOSITION AND *MAKES A FINE PET*

**NOAH WEBSTER** WHO PUBLISHED HIS FIRST DICTIONARY IN 1828, *HAD LABORED 21 YEARS TO COMPILE ITS 70,000 WORDS*

THE **JESUIT HOUSE** at Sillery, near Quebec, BUILT IN 1637 BY FATHER LE JEUNE, *IS THE OLDEST HOUSE IN CANADA.*

THE STRUCTURE BURNED IN 1657, BUT IT WAS REBUILT, USING THE SAME STONE WALLS, IN THE SAME YEAR

A **SNAKE BRACELET** WITH RUBY EYES WORN BY SARAH BERNHARDT IN CLEOPATRA IN 1890, COVERED MOST OF HER HAND AND PART OF HER ARM

## THEODORE ROOSEVELT

SHOT IN THE RIGHT LUNG BY A FANATIC DURING HIS 1912 CAMPAIGN FOR THE PRESIDENCY, MADE A CAMPAIGN SPEECH AS SCHEDULED A FEW HOURS LATER, SAYING: *"THERE IS A BULLET IN MY BODY, BUT IT TAKES MORE THAN THAT TO KILL A BULL MOOSE."*

## WILLIAM LLOYD GARRISON

(1805-1879) THE ABOLITIONIST, HAD TO BE JAILED FOR HIS OWN SAFETY ON OCT. 21, 1835, WHEN A MOB OF 2,000 TRIED TO LYNCH HIM IN BOSTON, MASS., FOR PREACHING THAT "ALL MEN ARE CREATED EQUAL"

**THE FARMER'S FRIEND** ONE OWL CAN CONSUME 10 MICE IN A SINGLE MEAL —WHICH CAN SAVE A FARMER AS MUCH AS 360 LBS. OF VEGETATION A YEAR

**THE MUSKET** LEWIS AND CLARK CAVERN, MONTANA, NATURAL ROCK FORMATION

**BATHTUB** IN JOHN PAUL JONES' HOUSE in Portsmouth, N.H., *HEWN FROM A MAHOGANY LOG*

**WIDOW'S WEEDS** WIDOWS AMONG THE PAPUANS OF NEW GUINEA, WEAR A BODICE AND BRIEF SKIRT *OF PLAITED GRASS*

**ELY SAMUEL PARKER** (1828-1895) WHO WROTE OUT THE SURRENDER DOCUMENT SIGNED BY GEN. ROBERT E. LEE TO END THE CIVIL WAR, WAS A SENECA IROQUOIS INDIAN

A **WOMAN** in Tibet, WEARS AN ORNATE HEADDRESS TO ADVERTISE THE FACT THAT SHE *HAS 2 HUSBANDS*

**CLARA BLOODGOOD** AN ACTRESS, COMMITTED SUICIDE IN 1907 BECAUSE HER COUNTERPART IN A LONDON PRODUCTION OF "THE TRUTH" RECEIVED BETTER REVIEWS

THE **BASILICA of SAINT-SERNIN** IN Toulouse, France, WAS UNDER CONSTRUCTION FROM 1060 UNTIL THE MIDDLE OF THE 12th CENTURY

A **PORTABLE SHOWER** INVENTED BY GASTON BOZERIAN IN PARIS, FRANCE, FOR TRAVELERS IN THE 1800's

THE **STUMP-TAILED LIZARD** of Australia, HAS A TAIL THAT LOOKS *LIKE ITS HEAD*

A **SMALL WOOD BUILDING** IN LITCHFIELD, CONN., IN 1784 BECAME AMERICA'S *FIRST LAW SCHOOL*

*The Legal Forger*

**SAUL WOLLMAN** of NEW YORK CITY, WAS SO EXPERT AT APING HAND-WRITING, THAT IN THE 1930's AND 1940's HE WAS HIRED TO SIGN THE NAMES OF 250,000 CELEBRITIES *INCLUDING BABE RUTH, JACK BENNY AND MAYOR LAGUARDIA*

**RICHARD OATES** A GOLD MINER AT MOLIAGUL, NEAR BALLARAT, AUSTRALIA, IN 1869 FOUND A NUGGET WEIGHING *142 POUNDS*

THE **MULE DEER** of California, HAS EARS **9 INCHES LONG**

THE **GROOM** in Bali, MUST HELP HIS BRIDE *COOK THE ENTIRE WEDDING FEAST*

**GENERAL BILLY MITCHELL** (1879-1936) WHOSE ADVOCACY OF AN INDEPENDENT AIR FORCE RESULTED IN HIS COURT-MARTIAL IN 1925, AS AN ARMY CAPTAIN, EARLIER IN HIS CAREER, *DEFEATED A PROPOSAL FOR A SEPARATE AIR CORPS*

**FLOYD COLLINS**
WHO DIED IN 1925 WHEN HE WAS TRAPPED WHILE SEEKING A KENTUCKY CAVE THAT WOULD MAKE A GOOD TOURIST ATTRACTION, BECAME A TOURIST ATTRACTION HIMSELF WHEN *HIS BODY WAS PLACED ON EXHIBITION IN CRYSTAL CAVE IN A SILVER CASKET*

**AINU GIRLS** of Japan MAKE THEMSELVES MORE CHARMING BY ADDING A *TATTOOED MUSTACHE*

THE **OLDEST LOG HOUSE IN AMERICA** DARBY, PA., A 2-ROOM STRUCTURE BUILT IN THE **1640's**

THE **STONEFISH** CONCEALS ITSELF IN A CREVICE-- *LOOKING LIKE ONE OF THE STONES*

**DOLLS** USED IN COLONIAL AMERICA *WERE OFTEN MADE OF TIN*

**THE CORACLE** A BOAT WELSH FISHERMEN MAKE TODAY BY STRETCHING CANVAS OVER A WOODEN FRAME, RESEMBLES THE VESSEL USED BY THEIR ANCESTORS *2,000 YEARS AGO*

**THE TOWER** OF St. Paul's Church in Eastchester, N.Y., HOUSES A BELL THAT IS THE EXACT DUPLICATE OF THE LIBERTY BELL IN PHILADELPHIA, PA., *EXCEPT FOR THE CRACK*

A **FRENCH PEASANT** IN THE 18th CENTURY, WAS REQUIRED TO PAY A TAX TO HIS LORD, A TITHE TO THE CHURCH, LAND, INCOME AND POLL TAXES TO THE KING, *AND FOR SEVERAL WEEKS EACH YEAR HAD TO WORK ON THE ROADS*

AN **ORNATE BATHTUB AND SHOWER** FRAMED IN CARVED MAHOGANY, ADVERTISED IN A LONDON, ENG., NEWSPAPER IN 1880

**NORBERT WIENER**
(1894-1964)
MATHEMATICIAN AND LOGICIAN,
LEARNED THE ALPHABET
IN 2 DAYS
*AT THE AGE OF
18 MONTHS.*
HE WAS GRADUATED
FROM TUFTS COLLEGE AT
14 AND RECEIVED
HIS PhD.
AT HARVARD
AT 18

**GUSTAVE FLAUBERT**
(1821-1880) THE FRENCH
NOVELIST FAMED FOR
"MADAME BOVARY," OFTEN
SPENT DAYS SEEKING
*A SINGLE WORD*

THE **GUAYRA WATERFALL**
ON THE PARANÁ RIVER BETWEEN
PARAGUAY AND BRAZIL,
AT EXTREME FLOOD HAS
*8⅓ TIMES MORE VOLUME
THAN NIAGARA FALLS*

**TRAVEL TRUNKS**
IN COLONIAL AMERICA,
OFTEN WERE CARVED FROM
*THE TRUNK OF A TREE*

**ALBERT PINKHAM RYDER** (1847-1917)
CONSIDERED ONE OF
AMERICA'S FOREMOST
PAINTERS, WAS AN
ECCENTRIC HERMIT
WHO LABORED
*20 YEARS ON
A SINGLE
PICTURE*

**GENTLEMEN**
IN THE 18TH CENTURY, DONNED AN APRON AND FACE MASK WHEN
*A SERVANT POWDERED THEIR WIG··OFTEN WITH A BELLOWS*

189

IRON WATCHTOWERS WERE ORIGINALLY BUILT THROUGHOUT NEW YORK CITY TO SPOT FIRES

BILL BRONTHON of PRINCETON UNIVERSITY AND GLEN CUNNINGHAM of KANSAS 2 RUNNERS WHOSE COMPETITIONS MADE TRACK HISTORY IN THE 30's, BOTH SUFFERED SEVERE LEG BURNS AS YOUNGSTERS-- CUNNINGHAM SO BADLY THAT HE WAS NEVER EXPECTED TO WALK AGAIN

E.E.CLIVE (1879-1940) A BRITISH CHARACTER ACTOR, PLAYED IN MORE THAN 100 HOLLYWOOD MOVIES IN A PERIOD OF 5 YEARS

THE WHITE-THROATED WOOD RAT ESCAPES ITS MORE TENDER-FOOTED ENEMIES BY RUNNING OVER CACTUS SPINES

AN INCOME TAX OF 2% ON ALL EARNINGS ABOVE $4,000 A YEAR WAS IMPOSED BY CONGRESS IN 1894-- BUT THE SUPREME COURT BANNED IT AS UNCONSTITUTIONAL

THE **ASTOR COLUMN** IN ASTORIA, OREGON, DEPICTS ON ITS 125 FEET THE HISTORY OF THE COMMUNITY --FOUNDED AS A FUR TRADING POST BY JOHN JACOB ASTOR IN 1811

GEN. **GEORGE S. PATTON** (1885-1945) EVENTUALLY BECAME AN EXCELLENT MARKSMAN, BUT IN THE 1912 OLYMPIC GAMES IN STOCKHOLM, SWEDEN, *HIS PISTOL SHOOTING WAS SO POOR THAT HE PLACED 5th IN THE PENTATHLON*

THE **SPRING PEEPER** THE SMALLEST OF ALL FROGS, *MEASURING ONLY ONE INCH*

THE **KEYHOLE STAIRWAY** IN THE KENTUCKY HISTORICAL MUSEUM AT FRANKFORT, *IS ENTIRELY SUPPORTED BY THE ARCHED STONE STEPS*

**THE OLD ARTS BUILDING** OF THE UNIV. OF NEW BRUNSWICK, at Fredericton, N.B., OPENED IN 1829, IS THE OLDEST UNIVERSITY STRUCTURE IN CANADA

**WILLIAM HENRY VANDERBILT** RICHEST MAN IN THE WORLD AT HIS DEATH IN 1885, WAS BURIED ON STATEN ISLAND, N.Y., IN A MAUSOLEUM THAT WAS INSPECTED BY A WATCHMAN EVERY 15 MINUTES TO *MAKE SURE HIS CORPSE WAS NOT KIDNAPED*

**HESSIAN SOLDIERS** IN THE AMERICAN REVOLUTION, TO MAKE THEM LOOK TALLER, *WORE HATS 18 INCHES HIGH*

**THE FRILLED LIZARD** of Australia, FRIGHTENS OFF PREDATORS BY REARING UP AND UNFOLDING A MANTLE **9** INCHES IN DIAMETER